The 2014 Elections
in Florida

The 2014 Elections in Florida

The Last Gasp From the 2012 Elections

*Patterns and Trends
in Florida Elections*

Robert E. Crew Jr. and
Mary Ruggiero Anderson

HAMILTON BOOKS
Lanham • Boulder • New York • Toronto • Plymouth, UK

Copyright © 2018 by
Hamilton Books
4501 Forbes Boulevard
Suite 200
Lanham, Maryland 20706
Hamilton Books Acquisitions Department (301) 459-3366

Unit A, Whitacre Mews, 26-34 Stannary Street,
London SE11 4AB, United Kingdom

British Library Cataloging in Publication Information Available
Library of Congress Control Number: 2017962168
ISBN: 978-0-7618-7012-8 (pbk. : alk. paper)
ISBN: 978-0-7618-7013-5 (Electronic)

♾️™ The paper used in this publication meets the minimum
requirements of American National Standard for Information
Sciences—Permanence of Paper for Printed Library Materials,
ANSI Z39.48-1992

Contents

List of Illustrations

FIGURE

TABLES

Preface

THE 2014 STATEWIDE ELECTION

In a real sense, the statewide elections in Florida in 2014 were a continuation of the stormy 2010 elections in the Sunshine State. Here's the connection.

In 2010, the popular sitting governor, Charlie Crist, resigned the position in order to run for a US Senate seat that was vacated before the term was up by Republican incumbent Mel Martinez. This move set off a "chain of events that led to a set of dramatic outcomes and to an unprecedented election" (Crew 2013, 3) in which the incumbent Republican Attorney General, Bill McCollum, was endorsed by his party's elite and quickly moved out to a lead in the polls over the Democratic candidate Alex Sink. However, Rick Scott, a former chief executive of a health care company who was frustrated by his inability to defeat the passage of the *Affordable Care Act* (U.S. Congress 2010) after spending $20 million of his own money attacking it directly, entered the Republican race with another contribution from his own bank account; this time it was $50 million. He secured the Republican endorsement in the primary, put another $20 million into his campaign from his own funds and went on to win the general election despite revelations of criminal investigations into his company, Columbia/HCA, and the payment of the largest fine for Medicare violations in the history of the program.

Crist, in the meantime, pursued his US Senate ambitions. He entered the Republican Senate primary as the heavy favorite, but was immediately challenged by the right wing candidacy of Marco Rubio and, when it became apparent that he would lose, withdrew to continue the race as an Independent. In a three way contest with Rubio and Democrat Kendrick Meek, Crist came in second to Rubio.

In 2014, Crist renewed his interest in the governor's office, changed his political affiliation again, this time to Democrat, and was eagerly endorsed by that Party's elite. He went on to win the Democratic primary and faced off against the person he had allowed to become governor when he resigned in 2010, Rick Scott, now running for reelection. While not the only person to run for high office in Florida as a candidate of both major political parties (see Jim Smith, 1979-1995) Crist certainly had the highest profile of any such individual. And no other person had ever run as a gubernatorial candidate under three separate designations on the ballot. This experience and visibility did not help him in 2014 and he lost to Scott by fewer than 65,000 votes in a race in which nearly 6 million were cast.

Further down the ticket, the Republicans also won all the other statewide races, including Secretary of Agriculture, Chief Financial Officer and Attorney General.

The Republican Party was not able, however, to take complete advantage of the normal off-year benefit that accrues to the party that does not hold the presidency, and as a result, did not add seats to its totals in the state's Congressional delegation or in the state Senate races. Republicans were successful in regaining six seats in the Florida state legislature. This book describes the nature of all of those campaigns and their outcomes.

Acknowledgments

From Mary R. Anderson: I would like to first thank my dear friend, mentor, and co-author Bob Crew. It has been a pleasure to work with you on this series that chronicles the elections in the state of Florida. I have learned a great deal about the state of affairs is this state, thank you for inviting me along for the ride. Thank you to Michael Harder, my student who gathered some of the data for the project. Finally, I would like to thank my family for their patience while I spent a good part of summer break writing (and missing out on the fishing). We spent many hours at the library instead but I think we can all agree that the Callicoon Library rocks!

Acknowledgments

Chapter One

The Race for Governor

In something of a continuation of the top of the ticket campaign in 2010, the 2014 race for governor included the primary figures from 2010 in different roles. The Republican candidate for Senate in 2010, Charlie Crist, became the 2014 Democrat challenger to the person who had become the Republican governor after Christ vacated that position to pursue a Senate seat.

THE CANDIDATES AND THE PRIMARIES

Republicans: Rick Scott had been elected in 2010 by the smallest margin of votes since 1876 when Democrat George Drew outlasted Republican Marcellus Stearns by 195 votes. He had gone on to serve four fairly undistinguished years during which he had never received a 50% approval rating from Floridians and in 2011, Public Policy Polling showed him to be one of the most unpopular governors in the nation (Kroll 2011). Nevertheless, he was the incumbent and no serious Republican candidates were willing to challenge him. Thus, it was left to two women with limited political experience to emerge to ensure that the Republicans had an alternative.

The first of these was Yinka Abosede Adeshina, a pharmacist who had worked for CVS and Scott's old company, Hospital Corporation of America. Although she had announced her candidacy for president in the upcoming 2016 election and was known to support health care for all Floridians by 2017, little else is known about her political proclivities (Bousquet 2014a). The *Tampa Bay Times* sent her multiple email and phone messages requesting campaign information and was unsuccessful in getting a response (*Tampa Bay Times* 2014a). She received 16,761 votes in the primary.

The second candidate was slightly more visible. She was Elizabeth Cuevas-Neunder who had filed to run against Jeb Bush in the 1998 Republican primary for governor but was forced to withdraw after her lieutenant governor candidate withdrew. She subsequently ran without success for the Sarasota County School Board in 2004 and the Florida House of Representatives in 2006. She was the founder of the Puerto Rican Chamber of Commerce for Sarasota-Manatee Counties, and of the Miss Latina Program, a mentoring program for Hispanic girls. Her political position included opposition to the legalization of medical marijuana because "hemp can do the same thing and can add a lot of jobs to the state of Florida" (*Tampa Bay Times* 2014a). She was also opposed to same-sex marriage and would have voted to increase the state's minimum wage to $10.10 per hour. She received 100,496 votes. In combination, the two challengers received 12.4% of the vote.

Democrats: Running as an Independent, Charlie Crist lost the 2010 US Senate race to Marco Rubio and many political commentators suggested that his long political career in Florida had finally come to an end. However, entreaties from the Democrats that had begun when he initially left the Republican primary continued after that loss, and he maintained contact with the leadership of the Party (see Crew and Anderson 2016, chap. 7 for the complete story). Crist went on to campaign for Obama in 2012 and was lured into a run for governor by Democrats who were reluctant to embrace their old adversary but who recognized his popularity and felt that he represented their best shot at defeating Rick Scott. In December 2012, he changed his party registration to Democrat claiming that "Republican leadership went off the cliff" (Whitaker 2014), and announced his candidacy in that Party's primary on November 1, 2013.

Crist's sole opponent in the primary was Nan Rich, former Democratic Senate Minority Leader and a representative in both the Florida House and the Senate for twelve years. A leader of the progressive wing of the Florida Democrats, Rich called herself the only "real Democrat" and spent the primary blasting Crist's apostasy on issues important to the Party's liberal base. She spent about $666,000 on the race (about ten times less than Crist) but after two and a half years on the campaign trail, she was never able to excite party faithful and ultimately succumbed to the former Republican by 74.6% to 25.4% of the vote (Bousquet and Caputo 2014).

THE GENERAL ELECTION FOR GOVERNOR: STRATEGIC CONTEXT

Off-year elections in Florida, as is the case throughout the nation, create a strategic environment that favors Republicans whose supporters typically turn out in higher numbers in these elections than do Democrats. Between 2000 and 2014, voter turnout in these elections was, on average, 25% lower than it was during presidential elections and, despite being outnumbered by registered voters over the time, Republicans won twelve of the thirteen state-wide races conducted during these years.

Well aware of their strategic advantage, the Republicans worked very hard to improve their numbers among registered voters and between 2010 and 2014 increased their registrants by 132,973 while the Democrats registration declined by a total of 2,890. Thus, when the election began, the Republicans had closed a 591,809 registration disadvantage in 2010 to a 433,946 deficit in 2014 (Florida Department of State 2017a).

At the same time, Governor Scott and his Republican colleagues in the state legislature worked to modify electoral laws in ways that critics claimed were designed to make it more difficult for traditional Democratic voters to participate in the elections. Changes adopted in House Bill 1355 in 2011 reduced the number of early voting days from fourteen to eight, greatly proscribed the activity of voter registration organizations like the League of Women Voters, and made it harder for voters who had changed county residence since the last election to cast ballots (Florida House of Representatives 2011). Research about the effects of these laws confirmed that "racial/ethnic minorities, registered Democrats, and those with no party affiliation had significant early voting participation drops and that voters who cast ballots on the final Sunday in 2008 [the "souls to polls" activity sponsored by African America churches] were disproportionately unlikely to cast a valid ballot in 2012" (Herron and Smith 2014, 646). All of these groups were heavily Democratic in party orientation and outrage at these efforts forced some modification of these laws in 2013. Nevertheless, critics claimed that the residual effects of these efforts lingered and inhibited electoral participation.

The condition of a state's economy is important to electoral outcomes and most models of gubernatorial elections show that positive performance in employment/unemployment is advantageous to the incumbent party. The 2014 election in Florida took place just as the nation's worst recession since the Great Depression of the 1930's had begun to recede, and restoration of jobs to the economy was the central issue in the campaign.

At its worst in 2010, just as Rick Scott was first elected, unemployment in the state had risen to 11.1% and was 1.5% higher than that in the nation as a whole. The rise in the rate corresponded with the gubernatorial term of Charlie Crist, and Mitt Romney and other Republicans in 2012 had been at pains to attack Barack Obama on the issue given that circumstance. However, when Crist left the Republican Party he was fair game for Scott and in 2014 the now-Democrat was left to defend his term as a Republican.

In his successful race in 2010, Rick Scott made economic recovery the central plank of his platform and promised to add 700,000 jobs to the Florida economy over the subsequent seven years. At nearly the same moment that Scott proposed this plan, Florida's nonpartisan Office of Economic and Demographic Research estimated that the state would add 1.05 million jobs over the succeeding eight years, regardless of who was in the governor's chair. In response to this news, Scott indicated that his 700,000 jobs would come in addition to those projected by the state economists, thus promising 1,700,000 jobs. In order to succeed, the Scott plan had to create more than 20,000 jobs a month on average for eighty-four months.

This goal was met only twenty-three times between 2010 and 2016, and Scott fell 1,000,000 jobs short of his target. Nevertheless, 700,000 jobs were created and unemployment in Florida fell from 11.1% in 2010, a rate that was slightly higher than the national average of 9.6%, to 5% at the beginning of 2015, the same as that in the nation as a whole. Thus, Scott argued he had "completely turned our economy around." Further, since Crist was now no longer a member of their Party, the Republicans were able to blame the recession and its loss of jobs during his term on him. Nevertheless, as the economy improved and Scott took credit for it, the issue became very awkward for the Republicans and during the 2012 presidential election "Mitt Romney asked Scott to tone down his statements heralding the improvement because it clashed with Romney's message that the nation was suffering under President Obama" (Abdill 2012).

As the 2014 general election began, Scott and Crist both found themselves in somewhat similar personal circumstances; for different reasons both suffered from a lack of enthusiasm within their own parties and both faced obstacles in their efforts to generate the kind of excitement that would produce high voter turnout.

The Governor's standing resulted from poor performance during his first term in office and from his awkward public persona. In the aftermath of Scott's near historic low margin of victory that had been facilitated by Tea Party support, he limped into Tallahassee in 2011, followed that party's hardline agenda for the first two years of his term and saw his approval ratings—even among Republicans—plummet. Between his election and the poll taken by the Quinnipiac Poll in July 2014, his average job approval rating was well below 50% (37.6 %) and he failed to receive majority support (50.1%) for performance in any of nineteen polls taken by that organization over the course of his tenure in office. His highest approval rating was 43% on June 18, 2013. In addition, in a poll taken in April 2014, 53% of the Florida electorate said he did not deserve re-election (Quinnipiac University Poll 2014).

On the personal dimension, Scott was described as "skull-faced a... nally awkward, and has been nicknamed Voldemort by his detractors" (Ball 2014). Tom Slade, the co-chair of his campaign and the former Chairman of the Republican Party of Florida, said "he doesn't seem to have any political skills at all. I give him a 'B' for governing. I'd give him an 'A' for strangeness" (Bender 2012).

Charlie Crist, on the other hand, suffered from high degrees of skepticism about his motivation in seeking the position as a Democrat. Although personally likable and a gifted campaigner, many Democrats remembered him as a self-proclaimed "pro-gun, pro-life" Ronald Reagan/Jeb Bush Republican" and Republicans saw him as a traitor. Rick Wilson, a GOP consultant, said of Crist, "he has all the intellectual horsepower of yogurt, but I admire his political skills. If Rick Scott could work a room like Charlie Crist, he'd be up by 25 points" (Terris 2014). Furthermore, Crist's relentless efforts to portray himself as a moderate in an increasingly partisan electorate limited his appeal both to the millennials who were registering with no party affiliation and who were generally progressive and to the 22% of liberals in the electorate.

POSITIONING, TARGETING, AND MESSAGE

The two candidates adopted positioning, targeting, and messaging strategies that were predictable given the circumstances in which they campaigned.

Recognizing his personal limitations as a candidate, Governor Scott abandoned almost all attempts to make himself more likeable and focused relentlessly on his management of the state's economy and on his attacks on his opponent. He positioned himself as the person who had brought Florida out of the financial despair that had gripped the state when Charlie Crist was governor, and whose leadership would ensure continued improvement in the economy. As stated in his first television advertisement, called "First Time," which first ran on March 25, 2013, "this is the first time in five years that our employment rate has been below the national average, but we're not stopping there."

As the campaign wore on, Scott moved beyond claiming responsibility for the recovery and blamed the recession on Crist and former Democrat Chief Financial Officer Alex Sink. He argued that Florida should have been immune to the recession and that "onerous state taxes and regulations in place before he took office *caused* Florida's job losses and his own pro-business governing formula ...has pushed Florida's recovery ahead of the nation's" (William March 2013). Although economic data, the Florida State's Office of Economic and Demographic Research and a number of economists suggested that these claims were "without empirical foundation," he was relentless in his portrayal of his "success" and repeated these talking points throughout the campaign.

The message adopted by Charlie Crist was more defuse and focused on the "disappointment and despair that I think this administration has brought on my fellow Floridians and our environment and our education and our ethics" (Farrington 2013). He promised to be on the side of average Floridians, "this time, all the time" and attacked Scott on a variety of class based issues. He bashed Scott's decision to turn down federal money for a high speed rail in central Florida and his refusal accept $10 million to expand Medicaid. He painted a portrait of Scott's Florida as "a state where the poor and middle-class are marginalized while opportunity is siphoned to powerful corporate interests and wealthy donors" (Mitchell and Monroe 2014). Appealing to a variety of progressive and human rights interests, he argued that "Floridians deserve a governor who fights for them – including for their right to marry the person they love and to be safe from discrimination in the workplace (Bloggytown 2014).

HOW THE REPUBLICANS CAMPAIGNED

The Scott Air War

Television commercials are undeniably the most effective way to reach voters in statewide political campaigns in Florida. With 12 million voters spread over a geographical area the size of a small country and divided into ten media markets of various sizes, candidates that cannot mount a serious and expensive television campaign are likely to suffer, especially if the opponent can do so. Given these circumstances, it was no surprise that the Scott vs. Crist battle played out largely through television advertising. Whether sponsored by the individual campaigns or by other organizations, the commercials were overwhelmingly negative, designed to disparage the opponent.

Rick Scott had seen the value of the medium in his 2010 race against both Bill McCullum and Alex Sink (where he spent over $70 million of his own money to win the Republican primary and the general election) and was prepared to replicate this effort in 2014. Ultimately, utilizing both his own fortune and contributions to his PAC, Let's Get to Work, Scott spent $68 million ($67.96 m.) on television in Florida, with a minimum of $1.1 million in each of the state's media markets (Caputo 2014).

Trailing Crist in the polls by double digits and suffering from a negative public image, Scott began his television campaign in March 2014 with a $2.2 million ad buy that highlighted his childhood with poverty burdened parents and the necessity of hard work on his part (Deslatte 2004). He followed this in early June 2014, by pumping nearly $13 million into the earliest ever blitz of attack ads in a Florida's governor's race. As of October 2014, he and his allies had launched 63,321 ads (Dunkelberger 2014). He concluded the final week of the campaign by running 4,000 ads, spending the equivalent of $1,200 a minute every day, every hour on television (Smith and Caputo 2014).

Adopting a scattershot approach featuring a dozen different ads, Scott flooded the airways. He put $6 million into Orlando on ads attacking Crist for tuition hikes at the state's public universities when he was governor. He also attacked the former governor for his support for the *Affordable Care Act*; he featured an ad in which a man who said he was swindled by a Ponzi schemer named Scott Rothstein who had been associated with Charlie Crist, and, therefore, by extension, had been swindled by Crist; he ran Spanish language ads titled "Nos Abandono." in which he talked about the number of jobs lost in Crist's term as governor; and in an odd ad featuring a woman who had yelled at Scott in a Starbucks coffee shop about the loss of her job, called her a "latte liberal" who sat around coffee shops demanding public assistance and claimed he had created a million jobs. He also ran some softer biographical spots showing him with one of his grandchildren.

By the end of the campaign, Scott had nearly doubled the amount of money spent on television advertising by Charlie Crist. The totals were $67.98 to $35.6 million in favor of Scott. He also out spent the former governor in all of the ten state's media markets, including the three where Crist won the most votes. The Republican Party of Florida added an additional $40.7 million in attack ads against Charlie Crist and $7.1 million in ads supporting Rick Scott (Florida Center for Public Integrity 2014). Reflecting on the size of the difference, one of Crist's strategists said, "it is very hard to run into a tsunami and go anywhere" (Smith and Caputo 2014).

The Scott Ground Game

Reflecting a long-standing Republican strategy in Florida, the gubernatorial campaign built upon the infrastructure of the Republican Party of Florida which, in turn, had been modeled on the Obama field organization. The Scott field staff was composed of individuals who worked for the Scott campaign and people who were engaged by the Republican Party of Florida. The campaign began nearly a full year before the election, opened forty-nine field offices, and claimed to have knocked on 2.1 million doors and made 2.7 million phone calls by October 2014 (Dunkelberger 2014). "He did a lot of things that needed to be done in the midterm election. . . . He invested very heavily and continued investing heavily in the ground game even a week or so before the election. He just never took his foot off the gas pedal" (Rumpf 2015).

In addition Scott employed a team of supporters who followed the Crist campaign closely, showed up at his campaign events, and either refuted and disputed the Crist message or offered criticisms about his proposals. The tactic, called "bracketing" is somewhat common in campaigns but was taken to new levels by the Scott campaign which had the resources to employ every possible campaign tactic. Democrats complained that "they have more money than they know what to do with, so they can afford to send people hither and yon" (Man 2014a).

Scott took "a statewide approach to campaigning," touring the state "on a different theme each week, using his family's plane to hit a different media market or two on each day. He also did a two week, statewide bus tour to promote his proposed tax cuts" (Associated Press 2014b).

HOW THE DEMOCRATS CAMPAIGNED

The Crist Air War

Charlie Crist ran the largest television campaign for governor ever run by a Democrat in Florida. By October, Crist had aired 30,340 individual ads (Dunkelberger, 2014), and by the end of the campaign he had spent $35.6 million dollars on this medium (Caputo 2014). This amount was nearly double the next largest sum ever spent on television by a Democratic gubernatorial candidate—Alex Sink in 2010—*but it was slightly less than half what his opponent put into television* (Crew 2013, 61; emphasis mine.).

As expressed through a variety of ads, Crist's television message contrasted his defense of and advocacy for the common Floridian with Scott's support for "greedy Wall Street bankers and corporate takeover artists." An ad entitled "Up Here," began with scenes of wealthy parts of Florida and explained that Scott was fighting for people in these parts of the state while he (Crist) was "fighting for you." In "Guys Like Rick Scott" Crist opens by saying that Rick Scott says I (Crist) am the guy who caused the recession but in reality it was Scott who supported guys like himself, wealthy, greedy people who wanted tax breaks and government subsidies for themselves. And in "Extreme" Crist attacked Scott for his extreme positions on issues of importance to women. Reflecting his targeting strategy, Crist spent most of his money in the Tampa Bay, Orlando, Palm Beach and Miami media markets.

Much of the research on the effects of television advertising on election outcomes focuses on the differences between candidates in the volume of ads produced and the amount of money spent on the ads. Michael M. Franz and

Travis N. Ridout have shown that an advantage of 1,000 ads over the month before the elections translates into an additional six-tenths of a point in a vote share (Franz and Ridout, 2010.). And John Sides and Lynn Vavreck show that an advantage of three ads per capita on Election Day translate into almost an additional point of vote share (Sides and Vavreck 2013). Given the closeness of the 2014 gubernatorial election, the advantage that Scott achieved over Crist in spending on television and on television ad volume in all likelihood explains the outcome of the race.

The Crist Ground Game

Crist tailored his ground game to improve turnout in the South Florida counties with high Democratic registration. About 1.5 million registered Democrats, or nearly 32% of these voters resided in Palm Beach, Broward, and Miami-Dade counties. Of the thirty-eight campaign offices Crist opened in the state, twenty-one were in these three counties (Associated Press 2014b). He also opened new offices in the Orange County community of Apopka, where 25% of the residents are Latino, and in other high African American and Haitian communities. Crist had "the biggest Get-Out-the-Vote effort for any Democratic governor's candidate in 20 years" (Nevins 2014). The campaign also profited from the ground game of the climate change activist group NextGen Climate Action, which opened twenty-one offices across the state and fielded an aggressive Get-Out-The-Vote effort across Central and South Florida that targeted voters likely to be sympathetic to Democratic candidates.

The campaign's primary target was Broward County, more populous than twelve American states and home to 545,000 Democrats. Traditionally the place where Florida Democrats had won statewide elections, voter turnout in the 2010 gubernatorial race had been only 41%, well below the statewide average of 49% for Democrats, and was the place where the Crist campaign staked its biggest election bet.

In the 1970s, Broward County was home to a large contingent of Jewish voters with a liberal bias. As this community passed on, the county was repopulated by a diverse mixture of African Americans, Haitians, Hispanics, and people from throughout the Caribbean who voted at lower levels than did the politically savvy Jews and who constituted a more difficult motivational target for the Dems. Thus, thirty paid workers were stationed in Broward County alone, spread among eight field offices (Bousquet 2014b), and the 73,000 African American voters who had supported President Obama in 2008 and in 2012, but who had stayed home in 2010 were identified and given special attention. Volunteers and paid staff called prospective voters who had been classified according to their likelihood to vote and/or to vote Democrat. Staff walked door-to-door throughout the county and high school students were hired on election day to track down voters who had not cast their ballot by then.

SUMMARY

Rick Scott's campaign manager surely must have thought that he had died and gone to campaign heaven when he realized that he was to be the director of a campaign that had access to virtually unlimited funds for its activities. These funds were the campaign's primary resource and the disparity between his funds and those of the Crist campaign was, without question, the primary factor that led to Scott's victory. Indeed, "Scott's late decision to put nearly $13 million of his own money into the campaign may have ultimately made the difference" (Smith and Caputo 2014).

Having said this, the Scott campaign did not win purely because it had more money than did his opponent. He made good use of the money. He bought television ads at strategic points during the campaign, he put resources into his ground game throughout the campaign, and he maintained message discipline throughout. In short, he played to his strength as the incumbent who had better funding than did his opponent and who had presided over an improved economy.

A campaign like that of Charlie Crist, losing an election by 1% of the vote, is invariably barraged with criticisms large and small, and the Crist campaign was the target of many. Some of these criticisms were farcical, others more substantial.

Starting with the ludicrous, political blogster Peter Schorsch, who named as the culprit "that logo! What was wrong with the sans-serif italics of campaigns past?" (Schorsch 2014b), suggesting that had the campaign changed its logo design electoral victory would have ensued.

A more substantial critique questioned the campaign targeting strategy and argued that Crist's very heavy focus on the Democratic strongholds in South Florida had deprived him of the resources that could have been put to use in other high percentage Democratic counties in Northeast Florida such as Gadsden, Jefferson, and Alachua. Although Crist won his targeted counties—Miami-Dade, Palm Beach, Broward–and outperformed the 2010 Democratic candidate in each, voter turnout was low and his margins in the south were not enough to overcome Scott's advantage throughout the remainder of the state. In the end, the Crist campaign simply was not able to motivate Democratic voters, and in particular the Hispanic, Haitian, African American, and Puerto Rican voters who had been the core of the Obama coalition.

Despite the loss, Crist campaign manager Omar Khan said that he was "comfortable with every strategic decision we made" (Smith and Caputo 2014), and Crist did engineer a strategically savvy and disciplined campaign. He created the first large field organization ever built for a Democratic gubernatorial campaign in Florida, and he opened nearly forty campaign offices in the state. He raised and spent the largest amount of money for any Democratic gubernatorial campaign in Florida history; however, he lost the election by fewer than 65,000 votes out of 5.95 million cast.

Chapter Two

The Gubernatorial
Election Results

On November 4, 2014, Rick Scott became only the second Republican since Reconstruction to win a second term as Governor of the Sunshine State (Smith, Bousquet, and Sanders 2014). The 2014 Florida gubernatorial election, which resulted in a narrow victory for Scott, was one of the costliest and most polarizing races for governor in Florida history. Voters were generally disenchanted with both candidates as demonstrated by their poor performance at the polls compared to the downballot candidates and ballot initiatives. For example, Rick Scott, received 488,000 fewer votes than did the successful candidate for CFO, Jeff Atwater; 477,000 fewer votes than Adam Putnam, Commissioner of Agriculture; and 357,000 fewer votes than Attorney General Pam Bondi. While Charlie Crist did run ahead of his downticket running mates, the vote totals for both gubernatorial candidates was 230,000 lower than that in the voting for the constitutional amendment legalizing medical marijuana.

Despite this lack of appeal toward both candidates, voter turnout was up in 2014 compared to 2010 from 49% to 51%, breaking the 50% marker for the first time in a midterm election since 2002 (Florida Department of State 2017c).

VOTE BY MAIL AND EARLY VOTING

Though voting by mail and early voting does not necessarily translate into votes for a particular candidate, current wisdom and previous research suggests that most voters tend to vote for the party with which they identify. This is particularly relevant for midterm elections, as midterm election voters tend to be the more fervent party loyalists. Democrats were riding a wave

Table 2.1. Vote by Mail and Early Vote Results

State Total	Republican	Democrat	Other	No Party Affiliation	Total
Vote by Mail (Absentee)	833,420	705,752	53,761	284,887	1,877,820
Early Vote	518,603	555,601	37,452	197,866	1,309,522

Source: Florida Department of State, 2014a, "2014 General Election, Election Number: 10218," http://dos.myflorida.com/media/696917/early-voting-and-vote-by-mail-report-2014-gen.pdf.

of optimism in the weeks preceding the election when early votes indicated that there was a small lead for the Democrats. However, Republicans cut that optimism with absentee ballots and strong Election Day turnout. The data displayed in table 2.1 shows that Democratic early voting was higher than Republican early voting, though Republicans more than made up any gains the Democrats had with absentee ballots. Overall, 3.2 million ballots were cast before election day, either through early voting or absentee ballot, and 2.8 million were cast on election day (and there were 12,593 provisional ballots cast). In the pages that follow we take a closer look at the gubernatorial race, examining the vote by county.

VOTER TURNOUT

In 2014, Rick Scott won fifty-four out of sixty-seven counties in Florida—two more than he did in 2010. The map below (fig. 2.1) indicates the counties that voted for Scott (shown in gray) and Crist (shown in black). Though Scott won 80% of the total counties, Crist won the counties with the largest populations. Among the five most populous counties, those with over 1 million people in each county, Crist won all five. Among the top ten most populous counties, Scott won only three (see table 2.2). Miami-Dade, the largest county, had the lowest voter turnout, just clearing 40%, and Union county, among one of Florida's smallest counties in terms of population (ranking sixtieth out of sixty-seventh) had the highest turnout at 72%. Among these population centers where Crist won, there was lower voter turnout than in 2010 with one exception, Orange County. This lower than expected turnout in the key counties of Miami-Dade, Palm Beach, and Broward—typically Democratic strongholds—resulted in a loss for Crist and all but secured the win for Rick Scott. As we show in table 2.2, none of the top five most populous counties broke a 50% turnout. The Obama coalition of 2012 failed to materialize for the midterm election in 2014. In addition, Scott did better than he had previously

Figure 2.1. Map of Scott and Crist Victories by County. *Source: CNN,* "America's Choice 2014: Election Center," November 6, 2014, http://www.cnn.com/election/2014/results/state/FL/governor/#.

Table 2.2. Top 10 Largest Counties by Population

Rank	County	Population	Turnout % 2010	Turnout % 2014	Winner 2014
1	Miami-Dade County	2,712,945	41.5	40.7	Crist
2	Broward County	1,909,632	41.0	44.5	Crist
3	Palm Beach County	1,443,810	47.5	49.2	Crist
4	Hillsborough County	1,376,238	47.7	49.1	Crist
5	Orange County	1,314,367	44.3	48.3	Crist
6	Pinellas County	960,730	51.3	57.2	Crist
7	Duval County	926,255	50.4	49.4	Scott
8	Lee County	722,336	53.2	52.5	Scott
9	Polk County	666,149	50.2	54.3	Scott
10	Brevard County	579,130	55.9	59.5	Crist

Source: Cubit, 2016, "Florida Demographics." Derived from the U.S. Census Bureau and Florida Department of State, Elections Division, "Annual Estimates of the Resident Population: April 1, 2010 to July 1, 2016," from http://factfinder2.census.gov. Available online at https://www.florida-demographics.com/counties_by_population.

Table 2.3.   Smallest Counties in Florida by Population

Rank	County	Population	Turnout % 2010	Turnout % 2014	Winner 2014
57	Gilchrist County	17,212	50.5	54.6	Scott
58	Dixie County	16,300	53.5	55.3	Scott
59	Gulf County	15,990	54.9	54.9	Scott
60	Union County	15,142	52.3	72.1	Scott
61	Calhoun County	14,423	51.8	51.0	Scott
62	Hamilton County	14,361	51.6	48.6	Scott
63	Glades County	13,970	42.9	51.6	Scott
64	Jefferson County	13,906	64.9	67.6	Crist
65	Franklin County	11,901	53.8	60.6	Scott
66	Lafayette County	8,617	58.1	59.9	Scott
67	Liberty County	8,202	52.6	60.7	Scott

Source: Cubit, 2016, "Florida Demographics." Derived from the U.S. Census Bureau and Florida Department of State, Elections Division, "Annual Estimates of the Resident Population: April 1, 2010 to July 1, 2016," from http://factfinder2.census.gov. Available online at https://www.florida-demographics.com/counties_by_population.

in several rural counties of north Florida (Smith and Caputo 2014). Turnout in the smallest counties increased with the exception of Hamilton and Calhoun counties—see table 2.3. Scott won nine out of the ten smallest counties save Jefferson County, which is adjacent to Leon County where Democrats tend to find success. Effectively, what we seem to have witnessed in the 2014 Florida gubernatorial election was a rural versus an urban divide, where urban voter turnout in Democratic-leaning counties decreased and rural voter turnout in Republican-leaning counties increased (the exception being Duval county, home to Jacksonville). In the following chapter we will dive deeper into group voting in the 2014 gubernatorial election.

The county by county results for turnout is displayed in table 2.4. It is evident that a majority of counties had greater than 50% turnout, however, this is not at all an impressive number when compared to general election turnout that tends to receive between a 70% to 75% turnout.

COUNTY BY COUNTY RESULTS

In only four counties did Crist manage to win more than 60% of the vote—Broward, Gadsden, Palm Beach, and Leon. Scott, however, won nearly 50% of the sixty-seven counties with greater than 60% of the vote (sixty-three counties in total). This overwhelming view of victories on a county–by-county level (table 2.5) is tempered by the state population centers, which

Table 2.4. Voter Registration and Turnout by County

County	Voter Registration	Turnout	% Turnout
Alachua	157,848	79,236	50.2%
Baker	13,948	8,619	61.8%
Bay	112,636	57,602	51.1%
Bradford	15,661	8,683	55.4%
Brevard	379,108	225,448	59.5%
Broward	1,067,083	474,620	44.5%
Calhoun	8,349	4,254	51.0%
Charlotte	120,030	68,101	56.7%
Citrus	97,335	59,158	60.8%
Clay	136,148	68,829	50.6%
Collier	187,982	114,931	61.1%
Columbia	35,464	18,599	52.4%
Desoto	14,939	7,629	51.1%
Dixie	9,939	5,501	55.3%
Duval	552,158	272,952	49.4%
Escambia	200,953	99,067	49.3%
Flagler	71,835	38,393	53.4%
Franklin	7,246	4,389	60.6%
Gadsden	28,990	17,708	61.1%
Gilchrist	11,099	6,056	54.6%
Glades	5,962	3,077	51.6%
Gulf	9,510	5,221	54.9%
Hamilton	7,765	3,770	48.6%
Hardee	10,998	5,485	49.9%
Hendry	16,616	6,788	40.9%
Hernando	124,800	64,925	52.0%
Highlands	60,515	32,508	53.7%
Hillsborough	765,993	376,306	49.1%
Holmes	11,123	5,815	52.3%
Indian River	97,947	53,495	54.6%
Jackson	28,116	15,292	54.4%
Jefferson	9,393	6,354	67.6%
Lafayette	4,464	2,673	59.9%
Lake	207,328	114,175	55.1%
Lee	405,730	212,913	52.5%
Leon	191,780	109,286	57.0%
Levy	25,877	13,497	52.2%
Liberty	4,483	2,723	60.7%
Madison	11,531	6,413	55.6%

(continued)

Table 2.4. *(continued)*

County	Voter Registration	Turnout	% Turnout
Manatee	212,609	121,098	57.0%
Marion	216,012	121,510	56.3%
Martin	105,248	62,489	59.4%
Miami-Dade	1,300,455	529,927	40.7%
Monroe	51,235	29,023	56.6%
Nassau	55,696	30,983	55.6%
Okaloosa	123,712	61,672	49.9%
Okeechobee	19,480	9,044	46.4%
Orange	723,401	312,925	43.3%
Osceola	167,672	69,304	41.3%
Palm Beach	852,211	419,459	49.2%
Pasco	304,868	162,736	53.4%
Pinellas	623,605	356,941	57.2%
Polk	358,332	194,723	54.3%
Putnam	45,153	22,976	50.9%
Santa Rosa	124,433	53,826	43.3%
Sarasota	277,296	163,427	58.9%
Seminole	266,005	147,384	55.4%
St. Johns	160,561	87,568	54.5%
St. Lucie	182,254	90,560	49.7%
Sumter	82,603	55,688	67.4%
Suwannee	25,049	12,905	51.5%
Taylor	12,109	6,764	55.9%
Union	7,171	5,167	72.1%
Volusia	330,613	178,442	54.0%
Wakulla	18,817	11,677	62.1%
Walton	41,778	20,594	49.3%
Washington	14,473	8,371	57.8%
Total	11,931,533	6,027,674	50.5%

Source: Florida Department of State, 2014b, *Division of Elections.* "Voter Turnout by County," https://enight.elections.myflorida.com.

we discussed earlier. Though Crist was unable to secure many counties, he won the counties that had the largest populations. In the chapter that follows we will turn our attention to the demographic composition of Florida voters, which helps provide a picture of the types of voters that each candidate attracted.

Table 2.5. County by County Results

County Name	Number of Votes		Percent of Vote	
	Rick Scott	Charlie Crist	Scott %	Crist %
Alachua	31,097	44,052	41.38%	58.62%
Baker	5,956	2,100	73.93%	26.07%
Bay	40,956	12,990	75.92%	24.08%
Bradford	5,525	2,594	68.05%	31.95%
Brevard	116,620	91,018	56.17%	43.83%
Broward	138,394	318,950	30.26%	69.74%
Calhoun	2,676	1,202	69.00%	31.00%
Charlotte	35,236	26,963	56.65%	43.35%
Citrus	31,305	22,424	58.26%	41.74%
Clay	49,330	15,948	75.57%	24.43%
Collier	75,337	35,281	68.11%	31.89%
Columbia	11,604	5,812	66.63%	33.37%
Desoto	3,681	3,294	52.77%	47.23%
Dixie	3,345	1,657	66.87%	33.13%
Duval	146,407	112,026	56.65%	43.35%
Escambia	60,719	33,434	64.49%	35.51%
Flagler	19,996	15,994	55.56%	44.44%
Franklin	2,505	1,633	60.54%	39.46%
Gadsden	4,798	12,425	27.86%	72.14%
Gilchrist	4,129	1,485	73.55%	26.45%
Glades	1,815	1,042	63.53%	36.47%
Gulf	3,476	1,432	70.82%	29.18%
Hamilton	1,958	1,622	54.69%	45.31%
Hardee	3,207	1,751	64.68%	35.32%
Hendry	3,749	2,626	58.81%	41.19%
Hernando	30,635	28,622	51.70%	48.30%
Highlands	18,888	11,070	63.05%	36.95%
Hillsborough	170,127	180,168	48.57%	51.43%
Holmes	4,301	1,052	80.35%	19.65%
Indian River	30,719	19,248	61.48%	38.52%
Jackson	8,745	5,711	60.49%	39.51%
Jefferson	2,840	3,291	46.32%	53.68%
Lafayette	1,710	752	69.46%	30.54%
Lake	63,009	42,811	59.54%	40.46%
Lee	121,962	79,454	60.55%	39.45%
Leon	38,289	66,739	36.46%	63.54%
Levy	8,408	4,172	66.84%	33.16%
Liberty	1,562	901	63.42%	36.58%

(continued)

Table 2.5. *(continued)*

County Name	Number of Votes		Percent of Vote	
	Rick Scott	Charlie Crist	Scott %	Crist %
Madison	3,131	3,024	50.87%	49.13%
Manatee	61,871	49,515	55.55%	44.45%
Marion	66,220	46,351	58.83%	41.17%
Martin	33,836	24,616	57.89%	42.11%
Miami-Dade	205,017	304,721	40.22%	59.78%
Monroe	13,096	14,305	47.79%	52.21%
Nassau	22,105	7,229	75.36%	24.64%
Okaloosa	46,162	12,129	79.19%	20.81%
Okeechobee	5,016	3,311	60.24%	39.76%
Orange	128,014	164,570	43.75%	56.25%
Osceola	29,431	35,457	45.36%	54.64%
Palm Beach	160,413	246,730	39.40%	60.60%
Pasco	75,222	72,363	50.97%	49.03%
Pinellas	144,271	183,930	43.96%	56.04%
Polk	98,224	79,481	55.27%	44.73%
Putnam	13,903	7,335	65.46%	34.54%
Santa Rosa	39,933	10,815	78.69%	21.31%
Sarasota	78,678	73,706	51.63%	48.37%
Seminole	73,355	62,786	53.88%	46.12%
St. Johns	58,150	24,921	70.00%	30.00%
St. Lucie	38,006	46,422	45.02%	54.98%
Sumter	37,633	15,867	70.34%	29.66%
Suwannee	8,445	3,597	70.13%	29.87%
Taylor	4,266	2,115	66.85%	33.15%
Union	2,780	1,905	59.34%	40.66%
Volusia	85,749	79,315	51.95%	48.05%
Wakulla	6,444	4,560	58.56%	41.44%
Walton	15,168	4,347	77.72%	22.28%
Washington	5,788	2,029	74.04%	25.96%

Source: Vote percentage for each candidate calculated as a percentage of the total votes casts by county. Florida Department of State, 2017a, *Division of Elections*, "Election Reporting System," https://results. elections.myflorida.com.

Chapter Three

Explaining the Outcome

Group Voting in the
2014 Gubernatorial Election

Incumbents rarely lose, even unpopular ones. In 2014 Florida was in the unique position of having two incumbents running for Governor. Rick Scott was the current governor and Charlie Crist was the former Republican governor turned Independent turned Democrat, and both were on the ballot. Though an unpopular governor, Scott ran on anti-Obama sentiment and eked out a victory against Charlie Crist. Crist was unable to turn out the vote or to create a solid coalition against Scott. In the pages that follow we take a closer look at the groups that supported each candidate, using exit poll data gathered by Edison Research for the Associated Press and other members of the National Election Pool which includes the major news networks ABC, CBS, CNN, FOX, and NBC (Associated Press 2014a; NBC News 2014).

GENDER, AGE, AND RACE

Patterns of previous elections held for the 2014 gubernatorial election. The Republican candidate won the support of men, whites, and older Floridians. The Democrat captured the support of women, African Americans, Hispanic or Latino voters, and younger voters. While Crist won the female vote 49% to 47%, Scott, won a majority of white women—57% compared to only 39% for Crist. Black women, however, overwhelming supported Crist—84% and Latino women supported him as well with 59%. Of African Americans, 85% supported Crist compared to 12% who supported Scott. Whites put their support behind Scott, giving him 58% of their vote compared to 37% for Crist. The Latino and Hispanic vote is a bit more nuanced. Crist won the Latino/Hispanic vote 58% to Scott's 38%. Among Cubans, 50% supported Crist compared to 46% for Scott, and 66% of "other Hispanic"—those who do not

Table 3.1.   Gubernatorial Vote by Gender, Race, and Age

	Charlie Crist (DEM)	Rick Scott (REP)	Total 2014	Total 2010	% Change 2010 to 2014
Gender					
Male	46%	49%	49%	45%	+5
Female	49%	47%	51%	55%	-9
Age					
18-29	51%	41%	14%	8%	+6
30-44	48%	47%	19%	17%	+2
45-64	49%	46%	42%	39%	+3
65 or over	40%	56%	25%	35%	-10
Race					
White	37%	58%	69%	74%	-5
Black	85%	12%	14%	11%	+3
Hispanic or Latino	58%	38%	13%	12%	+1
Asian	2%	—	2%	1%	+1
Other	2%	—	2%	2%	No change

Source: NBC News, 2014, "Decision 2014: Exit Poll Results," *NBC News*, n.d., http://www.nbcnews.com/
politics/elections/2014/FL/governor/exitpoll; and Robert E. Crew, Jr., *The 2010 Elections in Florida: It's the
Economy, Stupid!* (Lanham, MD: University Press of America, 2013).

considered themselves Cuban—supported Crist compared to 31% who supported Scott. There was also a divide between married and unmarried women in their support of the two candidates. Scott carried the married women vote with 55% compared to Crist's support of 42%. Unmarried women, however, voted for Crist with 54% compared to Scott's 41%. Crist won every age group except for those who were 65 years old and older. Thus, the winning coalition for Scott was white, married men and women over 65 years of age. This is a voting block that is reliable and whose turnout out tends to be higher, which is especially important in critical midterm elections, though Crist managed to capture the diverse groups that are growing in Florida. The percentage of white voters decreased in 2014 compared to 2010 while the percent of non-white voters increased. Similarly, the percentage of voters 65 year old and older decreased in 2014 compared to 2010 while the other age groups increased. Though these changes are slight, they nonetheless depict the changing electorate of Florida. These patterns can be seen in table 3.1.

EDUCATION AND INCOME

Extant research supports the hypothesis that lower income voters tend to vote for Democratic candidates. In the 2014 gubernatorial election, the results

Table 3.2. Gubernatorial Vote Choice by Income

Income	Charlie Crist (DEM)	Rick Scott (REP)	Total 2014
Under $30,000	54%	36%	17%
$30,000 to $49,999	48%	46%	23%
$50,000 to $99,999	49%	47%	35%
$100,000 to $199,999	44%	52%	18%
$200,000 or more	37%	63%	8%

Source: NBC News, 2014, "Decision 2014: Exit Poll Results," *NBC News*, n.d., http://www.nbcnews.com/politics/elections/2014/FL/governor/exitpoll.

of Florida voters continued to lend support this claim. Those whose family incomes were under $99,999 supported Crist, while those whose family incomes were over $100,000 supported Scott. As demonstrated in table 3.2, those in the lowest income category—those making under $30,000—supported Crist 54% to Scott 36%, while those in the highest income category—those making $200,000 or above—supported Scott 63% to Crist 37%.

The results of previous research suggest that education is associated with party choice but it is often a mediating variable that affects individuals differently; though the same can be said for gender, age, race, income, and the other variables we have already discussed. The data we have at our disposal, however, preclude us from developing a full model that account for all of these variables simultaneously. Thus, as has been done in previous editions of this book and what is typical of the presentation of voting results for the consumption of the public at large, we will present a simple crosstab of candidate vote choice by education level—see table 3.3. Scott carried the support of those with a high school degree, some college, and college graduates, while Crist carried the support of those with a postgraduate degree. As we demonstrated earlier, non-whites supported Crist and whites supported Scott. In table 3.4 we are able to demonstrate

Table 3.3. Gubernatorial Vote Choice by Education

Education	Charlie Crist (DEM)	Rick Scott (REP)	Total 2014	Total 2010	% Change 2010 to 2014
No high school diploma	—	—	3%	2%	+1
High school graduate	43%	51%	15%	20%	-5
Some college or associates degree	43%	51%	33%	31%	+3
College graduate	47%	49%	31%	32%	-1
Postgraduate study	55%	42%	18%	14%	+4

Source: NBC News, 2014, "Decision 2014: Exit Poll Results," *NBC News*, n.d., http://www.nbcnews.com/politics/elections/2014/FL/governor/exitpoll; and Robert E. Crew, Jr., *The 2010 Elections in Florida: It's the Economy, Stupid!* (Lanham, MD: University Press of America, 2013).

Table 3.4. Gubernatorial Vote Choice by Race and Education

Race and Education	Charlie Crist (DEM)	Rick Scott (REP)	Total 2014
White college graduate	41%	55%	36%
White college non-graduates	32%	61%	33%
Non-white college graduate	76%	22%	13%
Non-white non-college graduate	65%	30%	18%

Source: NBC News, 2014, "Decision 2014: Exit Poll Results," *NBC News*, n.d., http://www.nbcnews.com/politics/elections/2014/FL/governor/exitpoll.

vote choice by both race and education. The results are not surprising though given the changing demographics of the state, they are worthy of inclusion. Scott received a majority of support from both white college graduates and white non-college graduates, while Crist received nearly two-thirds of the vote from both non-white college graduates and non-white non-college graduates.

RELIGION

Countless studies have found religious affiliation in the United States to be strongly correlated with party identification and vote choice. According the 2014 US Religious Landscape Study conducted by Pew Research Center, the religious composition of adults in Florida is roughly 47% Protestant or other Christian, 21% Catholic, 3% Jewish, and 24% unaffiliated (religions 'nones') (Pew Research Center 2014). Given that we have access to some data on religion and vote choice in the 2014 gubernatorial election we would be remiss to ignore it given the strong association between the two. The data demonstrate

Table 3.5. Gubernatorial Vote Choice by Religious Affiliation

Affiliation	Charlie Crist (DEM)	Rick Scott (REP)	Total 2014	Religious Composition of Florida 2014
Protestant	39%	56%	52%	46%
Catholic	40%	57%	24%	21%
Jewish	—	—	3%	3%
Something else	—	—	7%	6%
None	65%	24%	13%	24%

Source: NBC News, 2014, "Decision 2014: Exit Poll Results," *NBC News*, n.d., http://www.nbcnews.com/politics/elections/2014/FL/governor/exitpoll; and Pew Research Center, 2014, "Religion and Public Life: Religious Landscape Study, Adults in Florida," *Pew Research Center*, n.d., http://www.pewforum.org/religious-landscape-study/state/florida/.

that among those who voted, 52% were Protestant or other Christian, 24% Catholic, 3% Jewish, 7% something else, and 13% none, note these figures are not that different than the figures from the Pew Research Center study described in table 3.5. Though there were not enough respondents in the exit poll to provide results for the categories Jewish, or something else, we do have data on the remaining categories. Scott enjoyed majority support of both Protestant and other Christians, and Catholics. While Crist had support of those with no religious affiliation; table 3.5 displays these results.

PARTY IDENTIFICATION AND IDEOLOGY

Party identification is the strongest predictor of how someone will vote in an election. People are reluctant to vote against their own party and thus split ticket voting is not the norm (voting for candidates of two different parties on the ballot, for example, a Republican for Governor and a Democrat for Attorney General). In 2014, despite the fact that Charlie Crist was a party switcher, the former Republican governor was able to secure 91% of Democrats, while Scott had the support of 88% of Republicans. According to the exit polls, Independents made up 33% of voters. They supported Crist over Scott (barely), but neither Crist nor Scott was able to get a majority of Independent voters. Crist obtained 46% of Independent voters compared to 44% for Scott. Thus, Scott's victory was likely attributed not to Independent voters, as it was in the previous election when he obtained a majority of independent voters (Crew 2013), but to the strong support (and turnout) of Republican voters.

The lens through which many people interpret politics is ideology. Opinions on issues are often associated with ideology, but the association between ideology and vote choice is not as strong as that between party identification and vote choice. True, conservatives tend to vote Republican and liberals tend to vote Democrat, but there is more movement in the numbers than we see with party identification and often those self-identified moderates are the swing voters. Among those who identified as liberals, 83% supported Crist

Table 3.6. Gubernatorial Vote by Party Identification

Party Identification	Charlie Crist (DEM)	Rick Scott (REP)	Total 2014	Total 2010	% Change 2010 to 2014
Democrat	91%	6%	31%	36%	-5
Republican	10%	88%	35%	36%	-1
Independent	46%	44%	33%	29%	+4

Source: NBC News, 2014, "Decision 2014: Exit Poll Results," *NBC News*, n.d., http://www.nbcnews.com/politics/elections/2014/FL/governor/exitpoll; and Robert E. Crew, Jr., *The 2010 Elections in Florida: It's the Economy, Stupid!* (Lanham, MD: University Press of America, 2013).

Table 3.7.   Gubernatorial Vote by Ideology

Ideology	Charlie Crist (DEM)	Rick Scott (REP)	Total 2014	Total 2010	% Change 2010 to 2014
Liberal	83%	12%	22%	19%	+3
Moderate	55%	40%	40%	42%	-2
Conservative	16%	81%	37%	39%	-2

Source: NBC News, 2014, "Decision 2014: Exit Poll Results," *NBC News*, n.d., http://www.nbcnews.com/
  politics/elections/2014/FL/governor/exitpoll; and Robert E. Crew, Jr., *The 2010 Elections in Florida: It's the
  Economy, Stupid!* (Lanham, MD: University Press of America, 2013).

compared to 12% who supported Scott. Of conservatives, 81% supported
Scott compared to 16% who supported Crist. However, among those who
identified as moderates, Crist was able to gain a majority of support, 55%
compared to 40% for Scott.

So, what was the winning coalition for Rick Scott? As we alluded to earlier, it appears that a strong showing of support and turnout by Republicans
secured the win for Scott. Scott supporters were typically older, white, Christian, and had family incomes over $100,000. Is this the same coalition that
supported gubernatorial candidates in the past?

VOTING COALITIONS IN ELECTIONS: 1998–2014

Our previous review of gubernatorial elections (Crew 2013) found that between 1998 and 2010 Democrats won majorities among women, liberals and
moderates, African Americans, the youngest voters (18-29), those with the
lowest family incomes, and both those with the lowest and the highest educa-
tional levels. Republicans, won majorities among men, whites, conservatives,
Latino voters, those with the highest incomes, and those with a college degree. Our findings suggest that there is not a specific office coalition (i.e., for
governor or senator), but rather a candidate coalition, one that centers around
a specific candidate. Thus, we found a Bob Graham coalition, a Jeb Bush coalition, and an Alex Sink coalition. In 2014, this pattern continues, we found
a Scott coalition made up of white, older, Christian, wealthier voters from
lesser populated counties. Crist tried to emulate the winning Obama coalition
of 2008 and 2012. While he captured the support of many of the same groups,
he failed to mobilize the coalition to turn out for him in the numbers needed
to win. His coalition of younger, non-white, urban voters materialized but not
enough of them to make up the gains Scott had with his coalition. By failing
to reach the necessary level of support from these groups, Crist was unable to
mount a victory against Scott, instead he handed him the executive office of
Florida for a second term.

Chapter Four

Issue Opinions and Candidate Choice

Gubernatorial Election 2014

Political opinions on publicly salient issues and candidate vote choice are often tied closely together. As we have established already, the single best predictor of how someone will vote is party identification. Party identification may act as a cue or as a shortcut for a variety of political opinions about contemporary political issues. For example, simply knowing a candidate is a Republican or a Democrat, a voter can surmise the candidate's position on a number of issues, such as healthcare, the economy, military interventions, immigration, and LGBTQ issues including same-sex marriage. Organizations such as Ontheissues.org and VoteSmart.org analyze public statements by candidates to create a profile of their positions on a host of issues. A review of candidate positions on key issues suggest that candidates typically adhere to the positions staked out by the national party (see table 4.1).

Past political science research has demonstrated a strong association between issue opinions and vote choice. In earlier chapters, we outlined the positioning, strategy, and messaging of the candidates (see chap 1). The candidates for the 2014 Florida gubernatorial election engaged one another in three debates. Voters anticipated that they would be able to gain knowledge about each of the candidates' positions on issues related to the campaign and the candidates' vision about the future of Florida. In the section that follows we will review data from the National Election Poll (NBC News 2014) that shed light on the relationship between political issues and support for candidates Rick Scott and Charlie Crist in the 2014 gubernatorial election. We conclude that adhering to party positions garners support for the candidate from the party faithful, and that candidates tend to highlight the issues that are most important to voters with messaging, positioning, and advertisements. In the final section of this chapter, we will engage the reader with a review of the

Table 4.1. Candidate Positions on Key Issues

Issue	Charlie Crist (DEM)	Rick Scott (REP)
Education		
Support increase funding for K-12 education	YES	YES
Support common core	YES	NO
Support school vouchers	NO	YES
Support increase funding for higher education	YES	NO
Elections		
Support increasing restrictions on campaign donations	YES	NO
Environment		
Support government action to limit greenhouse gases	YES	NO
Support government mandates/subsidies for renewable energy	YES	YES
Support development of high speed rail in Florida	YES	NO
Gay Marriage		
Support gay marriage	YES	NO
Gun Control		
Support gun restrictions	YES	NO
Healthcare		
Accept federal funds for Medicaid coverage	YES	Position has varied
Immigration		
Support colleges and universities awarding in state tuition rates to state residents who are not citizens	YES	YES
Marijuana		
Amendment 2 Legalize Medical Marijuana	YES	NO
Minimum Wage		
Support raising the minimum wage	YES	No position
Taxes		
Signed the Americans for Tax Reform Pledge to oppose any and all tax increases?	Unknown	YES
Support an increase taxes on corporations and/or high income individuals to pay for public services	Unknown	No
Voting		
Support automatic restoration of voting rights to ex-felons	Yes	No

Source: Campus Election Engagement Project, 2014, "Rick Scott vs. Charlie Crist: Nonpartisan Candidate Guide for Florida Governor's Race 2014," (blog), October 19, http://www.huffingtonpost.com/campus-election-engagement-project/rick-scott-vs-charlie-cri_b_5974442.html.

medical marijuana constitutional amendment ballot initiative that generated a flurry of advertisements and hype in the midterm election, but ultimately fell short of the supermajority—60% support—necessary to pass.

THE ECONOMY

The messaging and the positioning of the candidates suggests that the economy was a key issue in the campaign for governor in 2014. Data from exit polling confirm this point. Among the issues that voters were most concerned about, 45% indicated the economy, 20% healthcare, 16% illegal immigration, and 14% foreign policy.

Scott staked out his claim that he had turned around a failing economy left in place by Charlie Crist; and that he was the "jobs" governor and his five second soundbite "let's get to work" was a favorite on the campaign trail. Exit polls suggest Floridians, despite the gains touted by Scott, were nonetheless concerned about the state of the national economy. When asked "how worried are you about the direction of the nation's economy in the next year?" 73% responded that they were very or somewhat worried, while 25% were not too or not at all worried. Among those who were worried, Scott won a majority of support—58%. Among those who were not worried, Crist won 85% of their support. Like his Republican colleagues, Scott supports the belief that smaller government is better and business can be counted on to stimulate the economy. According to those interviewed when asked "Which is closer to your view: (a) Government should do more to solve problems or (b) Government is doing too many things better left to businesses and individuals," a majority of those who selected "b" supported Scott (73%), and among those

Table 4.2. MIP, the Economy, and Vote Choice

	Total	Charlie Crist (DEM)	Rick Scott (REP)
Most Important Problem			
Foreign Policy	14%	41%	54%
Health Care	20%	67%	28%
Economy	45%	48%	47%
Illegal Immigration	16%	24%	71%
Economy			
Very/Somewhat worried	73%	38%	58%
Not too/not at all worried	25%	85%	13%

Source: NBC News, 2014, "Decision 2014: Exit Poll Results," *NBC News*, n.d., http://www.nbcnews.com/ politics/elections/2014/FL/governor/exitpoll.

who selected "a" a majority supported Crist (81%). Thus, it would seem that adhering to key principals of the party allowed each candidate to garner the support of those who shared that belief. Given that 45% of those interviewed indicated the economy was the number one issue facing the country, it was a strong issue for both Scott and Crist to use in the campaign. Seemingly, Scott's position and message was the one that voters found most appealing.

HEALTHCARE

In a state with an aging population, healthcare typically ranks among the most important issues facing the country for Florida voters. Of those who ranked health care as THE most important issue, they supported Crist three to one; 67% voted for Crist compared to 28% who voted for Scott. On the one hand, Scott supporters believed the 2010 health care law went too far and 90% approved of the way Scott carried out the health care law. On the other hand, 18% thought the 2010 law was about right and 20% felt it did not go far enough. The 84% of those who disapproved of the way Scott carried out the 2010 law, supported Crist. In other words, those who disliked the *Affordable Care Act* (U.S. Congress 2010) (a.k.a. Obamacare) and approved of Scott's implementation of the law (i.e., joining a lawsuit against the Obama administration and failing to expand Medicare) supported Scott, and those who liked the *ACA* supported Crist. For a quick review of the health care implementation debate in Florida see Berman 2015. Again, we see that, similar to the economy, taking a position that is in line with the party's position, earns support for each candidate from the party faithful.

Table 4.3. Healthcare Opinion and Candidate Choice

	Total	Charlie Crist (DEM)	Rick Scott (REP)
Do you think the 2010 federal health care law:			
Did not go far enough	20%	72%	20%
Was about right	18%	76%	20%
Went too far	47%	20%	75%
How do you feel about the way Rick Scott has carried out the 2010 federal health care law?			
Approve	38%	5%	90%
Disapprove	45%	84%	11%

Source: NBC News, 2014, "Decision 2014: Exit Poll Results," *NBC News*, n.d., http://www.nbcnews.com/politics/elections/2014/FL/governor/exitpoll.

SOCIAL ISSUES

The most polarizing election issues tend to be social issues. We take a quick look at two such issues: same-sex marriage and immigration; and their influence on support for Crist and/or Scott. Advocates of same-sex marriage won a victory in the courts in June 2015 when the US Supreme Court ruled in *Obergefell et al. v. Hodges* that same-sex marriage was legally protected in all fifty states by a vote of five to four. However, just a mere eight months prior to the ruling in November 2014, the voters of Florida were divided on the issue. While same-sex marriage was not considered to be among the most important issues for voters, it does ignite mobilization on both sides of the political spectrum. In fact, the exit polls show that voters were evenly split 48% to 48% on whether the state should recognize same-sex marriage. Among those who supported a recognition of same-sex marriage, 71% supported Crist, while those who did not support same-sex marriage—69% supported Scott. This follows the same pattern of party position taking by candidates that we reviewed earlier.

Hispanics are the largest minority in the state of Florida. They make up 20.5% of Florida's population, or nearly one in four Floridians. The state of Florida has a growing Latino/Hispanic population. The I-4 corridor which extends from Tampa to Orlando has experienced a population boom from those migrating to escape an ailing economy in Puerto Rico. Still, the largest Hispanic community remains Cuban Americans with just over 1 million in the state of Florida. Hispanics are growing in the Florida electorate, 13.9% of active registered voters in Florida are Hispanic. Democrats increased participation by Hispanics in the party by 26% in the 2012 election and Republicans

Table 4.4. Marriage Equality, Immigration Opinion, and Candidate Choice

	Total	Charlie Crist (DEM)	Rick Scott (REP)
Same-Sex Marriage: Should your state legally recognize same-sex marriage?			
Yes	48%	71%	25%
No	48%	29%	69%
Immigration: Should most illegal immigrants working in the US be:			
Offered a chance to apply for legal status	53%	61%	33%
Deported to the country they came from	36%	24%	71%

Source: NBC News, 2014, "Decision 2014: Exit Poll Results," *NBC News*, n.d., http://www.nbcnews.com/politics/elections/2014/FL/governor/exitpoll.

gained 7% in registrations by Hispanics, but the fastest growth was among no-party affiliation at 38%. Thus, both parties have much to gain by courting this group of voters (Vogel 2013). However, white voters remain a dependable and solid constituency, particularly for Republican candidates. This is not an easy needle for candidates to thread. Immigration is important to Hispanic voters but they are equally concerned about education, healthcare, and the economy. For a quick look at opinion about immigration we can turn to the National Exit Poll (NBC News 2014). Exit polls asked "should most illegal immigrants working in the United States be: (a) offered a chance to apply for legal status, or (b) deported to the country they came from." Responses that they should be offered a chance to apply for legal status was 53%, while 36% responded that they should be deported. Among those who selected option "a"—chance for legal status, Crist won 61% support. Among those who selected option "b"—deportation, Scott won 71%.

THE OBAMA EFFECT

Popular presidents can often lend their support to help candidates in close elections. However, some of President Obama's lowest approval numbers, those close to 40% nationally, were in 2014, particularly in the months leading up to the midterm election (Topaz 2014; Gallup n.d.). This was untimely for Democratic candidates across the United States, particularly Charlie Crist who was in the political battle of his life, but it worked to the advantage of Rick Scott. Obama could be a polarizing figure and was fairly unpopular with

Table 4.5. Obama Approval and Vote Choice

	Total	Charlie Crist (DEM)	Rick Scott (REP)
Obama Job Approval			
Strongly approve	22%	96%	3%
Somewhat approve	20%	80%	15%
Somewhat disapprove	16%	48%	46%
Strongly disapprove	41%	12%	85%
Feelings about Obama Administration			
Enthusiastic	6%	—	—
Satisfied, but not enthusiastic	31%	21%	75%
Dissatisfied, but not angry	38%	52%	42%
Angry	21%	79%	15%

Source: NBC News, 2014, "Decision 2014: Exit Poll Results," *NBC News*, n.d., http://www.nbcnews.com/politics/elections/2014/FL/governor/exitpoll.

Florida voters (Man 2014b). Thus, it is worthwhile to take a look at the approval/disapproval numbers for Obama and candidate vote choice. Scott after all, ran a fairly strong anti-Obama campaign and message.

Of those interviewed in exit polls, 57% disapproved of President Obama's handling of his job as President while 42% approved. Among those who approved, Crist secured 88% support. Of those with an unfavorable job approval of President Obama, Rick Scott enjoyed 74% support. In terms of feelings more generally about the Obama administration, a whopping 61% had negative feelings (dissatisfied or angry) compared to 38% who had positive feelings (enthusiastic or satisfied). Scott enjoyed the support of 75% of those who had negative feelings towards the administration and Crist easily captured 87% of those with positive feelings. Thus, we may conclude that there was indeed an *Obama effect*, one that helped Scott but likely hurt Crist.

MEDICAL MARIJUANA AMENDMENT 2

It was one of the most expensive ballot initiatives the country had ever witnessed. The battle to legalize medical marijuana in Florida was lost by a narrow margin in 2014. Constitutional ballot initiatives in the state of Florida requires that a supermajority of 60% vote YES for the measure to be enacted.

It is estimated that close to $12 million was spent on the campaign by opponents and supporters of the measure. Opponents were backed by Las Vegas billionaire Sheldon Adelson; they spent approximately $6 million in a campaign to defeat the ballot initiative. Drug Free Florida which opposed the measure and created the VOTE NO on 2 campaign, issued warnings to voters that the loose wording of the initiative would lead to "defacto legalization of marijuana" (Cordiero 2016). The official wording of the ballot initiative is state below:

> Allows the medical use of marijuana for individuals with debilitating diseases as determined by a licensed Florida physician. Allows caregivers to assist patients' medical use of marijuana. The Department of Health shall register and regulate centers that produce and distribute marijuana for medical purposes and shall issue identification cards to patients and caregivers. Applies only to Florida law. Does not immunize violations of federal law or any non-medical use, possession or production of marijuana. (Ballotpedia 2014)

Supporters of the initiative had the backing of celebrity lawyer John Morgan and countered with nearly $7 million spent in a campaign to legalize medical marijuana. People United for Medical Marijuana marketed a message of compassion for patients suffering from debilitating diseases such as

Table 4.6.   Amendment 2 Medical Marijuana and Vote Choice

Allow the use of medical marijuana	Total	Charlie Crist (DEM)	Rick Scott (REP)
YES	59%	62%	32%
NO	41%	27%	70%

Source: NBC News, 2014, "Decision 2014: Exit Poll Results," *NBC News*, n.d., http://www.nbcnews.com/
   politics/elections/2014/FL/governor/exitpoll.

cancer, MS, ALS, HIV, Crohn's, and Parkinson's (Associated Press 2014c). Republican law makers tended to oppose the measure while Democrats supported it. Political pundits predicted that having the measure on the ballot would help Democrats, particularly Charlie Crist, as the measure had the strongest support among young voters and they predicted turnout would increase among this demographic in the midterm election. However, Charlie Crist lost and the measure fell just short of passage. There were 57% who voted YES, while 42% voted NO. Supporters vowed to continue the fight noting that a majority of Floridians supported legalizing medical marijuana. Ben Pollara for United for Care tweeted just two days after the election on November 6, 2014 "#YesOn2 got a higher % of the vote than the last 6 Florida governors including Jeb Bush in his 2002 landslide." Politifact rated the tweet as "mostly true" (Gillin 2014).

Exit poll results demonstrate that Crist won a majority of those who voted YES for Amendment 2—allowing the medical use of marijuana and Scott won a majority of those who voted NO (see table 4.6).

Overall, the issue opinions we have discussed highlight that voters tend to support the same policies that the candidate of their choice supports. It is not possible with this data to determine causality, whether individual issue positions lead to candidate vote choice, but clearly there is a relationship between candidate positions on issues and individual positions on issues. Republican voters support the same issues as Republican candidates as do Democrats. In the case of the 2014 gubernatorial election, both Crist and Scott adopted the positions of the national party on the most publically salient issues and they won the support of those who agreed with them on the issues. Finally, Obama's popularity, or lack thereof in Florida, was likely a contributing factor for Crist's loss. As we discussed in chapter 3, turnout was lackluster for Democrats and we might conclude that part of that was related to Obama's low approval numbers.

Chapter Five

The Campaigns for
the Constitutional Offices

In addition to the Governor and Lieutenant Governor, the citizens of Florida also elect three other offices in the 2014 statewide elections, Commissioner of Agriculture and Consumer Services, Chief Financial Officer, and Attorney General (AG). These officials are independently responsible for the administration of the Departments of Agriculture, of Financial Services and of Legal Services.

While many, if not most, states select some executive branch officials in separate elections, Florida is the only state in the nation to use these individuals in a unique cabinet system in order to manage its executive branch of government. In Florida, these officials join the governor in a four person Florida Cabinet that has jurisdiction over twelve other state agencies that include:

- State Board of Executive Clemency
- State Board of Administration (excluding the Commissioner of Agriculture)
- Division of Bond Finance
- Department of Veterans' Affairs
- Department of Highway Safety and Motor Vehicles
- Department of Law Enforcement
- Department of Revenue
- Administration Commission
- Florida Land and Water Adjudicatory Commission
- Electrical Power Plant and Transmission Line Siting Board
- The Board of Trustees Internal Improvement Trust Fund
- Financial Services Commission

Table 5.1. 2014 Elections for Florida Constitutional Office

Office	Democrats	Republicans
Governor	2,801,198	2,865,343
Attorney General	2,457,317	3,222,524
Chief Financial Officer	2,337,727	3,535,897
Commissioner of Agriculture and Services	2,356,178	3,342,392

Source: Calculated by author from data at Florida Department of State, 2017b, *Division of Elections*, http://dos.myflorida.com/elections.

In biweekly meetings chaired by the governor, this Cabinet discusses agency business and makes policy decisions for these twelve agencies. The existence of this cabinet reflects the state's paranoia about the concentration of power in the hands of a single individual.

In spite of their important role in the management of Florida's government, elections for these offices routinely draw much less attention than does that of the governor, and the voter turnout for them is typically much lower than is that for the governor. However, for the first time in the 2010 cycle and again in the 2014 election in Florida, all three of the Republican downticket candidates ran ahead of that party's gubernatorial candidate, Rick Scott. In this portion of the book, we explore the nature of these campaigns and seek an explanation for the unusual circumstances in the race.

In 2010, for the first time in the state's history, none of these offices had incumbents seeking re-election and as a result there were hotly contested races in both of the parties' primaries and in the general election (see Crew 2013, 85-102). In 2014, the opposite circumstances emerged (i.e., incumbents held all three positions, there was only one primary contest and the general election pitted established incumbents against marginal challengers). The results of the races are shown in table 5.1.

THE RACE FOR ATTORNEY GENERAL

The AG in Florida, as is the case in most states, is considered one of the most influential and powerful public officials in the state. As Florida's chief law enforcement officer, the AG directs the state's Department of Legal Affairs, defends the constitutionality of state statues, and issues formal legal opinions on issues of state law. The Office of the AG is specifically responsible for protecting Florida consumers from various types of misconduct, for pursuing cases of Medicaid fraud, for defending state agencies in civil litigation cases,

Her campaign was fairly typical for a statewide office. It was conducted primarily through television advertisements that promoted her fight against prescription drug abuse, and through direct mail and messages sent via social media. Supported by $2.2 million from the Republican Party, Bondi raised over $4 million for her campaign, overwhelming her opponent.

The George Sheldon Campaign

George Sheldon came into the race as an experienced public official and a seasoned campaigner. He had been a deputy AG and could challenge his opponent with his knowledge of the office. Unfortunately for him, he could not raise enough money to become a viable candidate.

The Florida Democratic Party went "all in" on the gubernatorial race, leaving no resources for other candidates, no outside groups stepped in on his behalf and he was not, like the Republican gubernatorial candidate, personally wealthy.

The only serious external money brought into the campaign came in the form of an attack ad against Bondi (and three other state AGs) by former New York City mayor Michael Bloomberg for their suit against the Obama administration over new regulations on carbon emissions from power plants. In Florida the ads called Bondi "an attorney general for polluters, not for us" (Haberman 2015).

In addition to this Bloomberg campaign, the Sheldon organization raised $898,817, less than one quarter of the Bondi total, and he was unable to mount a television ad campaign, a death blow for a statewide campaign in Florida if the opponent could do so.

The money the campaign did raise went almost exclusively to direct mail and to social media campaigns that attacked Bondi for the positions she took on the issues described earlier. The campaign also tried to promote stories about two other incidents in Bondi's history: (1) her involvement with Donald Trump regarding Trump University; and (2) her effort to reschedule an execution in order to attend a campaign fundraiser.

The Trump University kerfuffle has become a part of Bondi's legacy in Florida. In 2012, New York's AG Eric Schneiderman brought a lawsuit against *the Donald* for fraudulent advertising regarding the education to be received at his "university." Although some of the complaints against the Trump University were lodged by Florida residents, Bondi refused to join the lawsuit, and ultimately Bondi never did investigate Trump University. New York's Schneiderman did and sued on behalf of the students. While Trump denounced the lawsuits as meaningless, he subsequently settled with Schneiderman and paid $25 million in restitution, some of which went to Florida residents, but none of their cases were handled by Bondi (Auslen 2016).

In the aftermath of this settlement, it was discovered that Trump had donated $25,000 from his foundation to Bondi's re-election campaign. Although Bondi held a tense news conference saying "I would never, ever, trade any campaign donation for some type of favor to anyone," the issue still has resonance in Florida (Kam 2014; Bousquet and Auslen, 2016).

A second issue that became a focus in the campaign was an attempt on the part of the Bondi campaign to delay the execution of a convicted murderer so that Bondi could attend a Tampa fundraiser for her campaign. Bondi told the governor's office that she had a conflict with that date, but did not report the nature of the conflict and Scott rescheduled the event. While the Sheldon campaign fumed about the hypocrisy of the request given Bondi's position as a strong supporter of the death penalty, it did not affect the outcome of the race and, as shown in table 5.1, she defeated Sheldon by 765,207 votes, or a 13% margin.

THE RACE FOR CHIEF FINANCIAL OFFICER

The Chief Financial Officer (CFO) of Florida is a statewide constitutional officer created in 2002. The CFO is also the director of two other state offices: Comptroller and Treasurer/Insurance Commissioner/Fire Marshal. The office heads the Florida Department of Financial Services and is responsible for overseeing the state's finances, collecting revenue, paying state bills, auditing state agencies, regulating cemeteries and funerals, and handling fires and arsons. In addition, the CFO has administrative oversight of the offices that handles banking and insurance regulation. The CFO, like the AG is a member of Florida's Cabinet.

In 2014, the incumbent CFO was Republican Jeff Atwater, a former President of the Florida Senate who had been first elected in 2010. His Democratic opponent was Will Rankin, a veteran of the US Army who had worked at the Ohio treasury department and was a former Republican.

From the outset, this race was no contest. Atwater raised $4.2 million; Rankin raised $35,636. Atwater ran television ads that said he was "the state official who arrests people for fraud and 'who protects the state's most vulnerable citizens from financial harm and abuse' and Rankin said Atwater supported insurance companies and big business, not the average Floridian" (Lush 2014), but no one heard this directly from his campaign since his resources did not permit him to run one. His vote came as a function of

Democrats voting the straight party ticket and many fewer of these citizens voted than did Republicans.

In the election where more Floridians cast a ballot than in any other in 2014, Atwater defeated Rankin by 1.1 million votes (table 5.1).

THE RACE FOR THE COMMISSIONER
OF AGRICULTURE AND CONSUMER SERVICES

The position of Commissioner of Agriculture and Consumer Services in Florida began life in 1868 as the Commissioner of Immigration and was tasked with encouraging farmers to settle in the State. In 1885 it was renamed Commissioner of Agriculture and given responsibility for supporting and promoting Florida's agricultural industry. In 1967 the Department was also given responsibility for overseeing the state's efforts to protect Florida's consumers, and in 1969 it became officially the Florida Department of Agriculture and Consumer Services. According to its website, "our programs and activities are so varied and extensive, they touch the life of just about every Floridian" (Florida Department of Agriculture and Consumer Services 2017).

In 2014, the incumbent in this position was Adam Putnam, whose adult life had been spent as an elected official and who had been a member of the US Congress before running for Agriculture and Consumer Services Commissioner. Putman was first elected as Commissioner in 2010. His Democratic opponent in the 2014 race was Thaddeus "Thad" Hamilton, who had worked for thirty-six years for the US Department of Agriculture. Thad had also been a member of the Broward County Land Preservation Advisory Committee as well as the South Florida Ecosystem Restoration Task Force.

As was the case with the race for CFO, the race for Commissioner of Agriculture was not a real contest. Putnam raised $3.8 million and Hamilton raised $38,251. This advantage gave Putnam the ability to advertise on television, to campaign around the state on a bus, and to exhibit a strong presence on Twitter. Hamilton, on the other hand, was reduced to making statements such as "we have to get away from money. Money should not be a key qualifier in this" and hoping someone heard him. Unfortunately, money was the qualifier and Hamilton could not overcome his lack of it. As shown in table 5.1, he lost by nearly 1 million votes.

Chapter Six

The Congressional Campaign

In the aftermath of the 2010 US Census, the State of Florida was awarded two additional congressional seats and was required to redraw the congressional district boundaries to reflect one-person-one-vote principals. The Republican majority in the Florida state legislature used its influence in this process to design both state legislative and congressional districts in a manner that was clearly biased in their favor. The Florida chapter of the League of Women Voters sued for redress on this issue, but it was not until July 2014 that the court made a decision, saying "what is clear to me from the evidence is ... that the group of Republican political consultants did in fact conspire to manipulate and influence the redistricting process ...with improper partisan intent and made a mockery of the rules of transparency in the process" (La-Fauci 2014). However, in the meantime, the 2012 congressional elections were held and Republicans won nineteen of the available twenty-seven seats (See Crew and Anderson 2016, 67-83, for an analysis of these elections), and audaciously sought to postpone drawing a new map until after the 2014 election, thus preserving their undeserved influence for an additional two years. Finally, after a Leon County Circuit Judge again ordered redistricting, a special legislative session was called, and on August 11, 2014 a new map was drawn that altered seven of the state's congressional districts and paved the way for new districts. In a subsequent ruling, a state circuit court judge ruled that the existing districts could stand for the 2014 elections (Klas 2014). In the following paragraphs, we describe the outcomes of the races involved.

District 1

Florida Congressional district 1 is the westernmost district in the state, stretching from Pensacola to the Alabama border. It includes Washington, Holmes,

43

and Walton counties. It is home to Elgin Air Force Base and the Pensacola Naval Air Station as well as Emerald Coast beach destinations at Destin and at Fort Walton Beach. It has more military veterans as residents than any other congressional district in the country (Leary 2014).

Long a solid Democratic seat, the first district cut ties with the presidential wing of that party in the 1960s and has not cast a majority vote for a Democratic presidential candidate since John F. Kennedy. Nevertheless, it continued to vote for Democratic congressional candidates until *MSNBC*'s "Morning Joe" Scarborough was elected as its first Republican in 1994. It has voted Republican since that time and, according to the Cook Partisan voting index (PVI), is the state's most Republican district. Cook's PVI also ranks it the twenty-first most Republican district in the nation with a PVI of R+21 (Cook's PVI is calculated by comparing the district's average Democratic or Republican Party's share of the two-party presidential vote in the previous two elections to the nation's average share of the same vote. In this case, the Republican congressional candidate received 21% more votes than did the Republican presidential candidate) (Cook Political Report, cookpoliticalreport@cookpolitical.com).

The incumbent, Jeff Miller, was a former Democrat who became a Republican in the late 1990s with the mass conversion of southern conservative Democrats to the GOP in reaction to Democratic support for the Civil Rights movement. Miller has one of the most conservative voting records in the US House of Representatives.

Given his seniority and the district's partisan composition, one might expect Republicans to run unopposed. Nevertheless, for six of the past eight years the Democrats have mounted a challenge by supporting James Bryan, a former US Army First Sergeant who had earned the Bronze Star with a V for Valor, a Silver Star for Valor, and a Purple Heart for wounds sustained in combat. In his races as a Democrat, Mr. Bryan won an average of 26.7% percent of the vote and in the 2014 race was defeated by 76.5% to 23.4%. (All vote totals and percentages taken from the website of the Florida Department of State, Division of Elections, *myFlorida.com*).

District 2

Florida's second congressional district is composed of twelve complete counties and parts of two others. These counties are stretched over the central and western portions of the Florida panhandle and are viewed as the classic old South, with "cotton fields, soft pine stands, catfish farms, large families, small towns with large churches" (Barone and Cohen 2004, 393). Voter registration favors the Democrats, but many of these voters left the Party philosophically long ago and regularly vote for Republican candidates, and in 2010 it had elected its first Republican in decades, Steve Southerland. (Florida Division of Elections, 2014c) As the 2014 race began, most of the nation's prominent political analysts, Sabato's *Crystal Ball*, *Fair Vote*, and the *Cook Political Report*, rated the district as a "likely" Republican district or as a "leaning Republican" district.

Republican success had begun when the Democratic Party's seven term Blue Dog incumbent, Alan Boyd, lost his seat in the *wave* election of 2010. In that race a combination of a poor economy, unhappiness with President Obama, and some courageous votes on the incumbent's part for the *Affordable Care Act* (U.S. Congress 2010), and other legislation fraught with partisan implications gave undertaker Steve Southerland, a first time Republican candidate from Panama City who had Tea Party backing, a 12.2% victory. Subsequently, he had served in Congress as a polarizing, right wing ideologue who was re-elected by 5% of the vote in 2012

Despite two consecutive victories by a Republican, the district remained on the Democratic Congressional Campaign Committee's "Red To Blue List" which identifies districts around the nation that the Democrats have targeted to flip from Republican to Democratic control. There were, as of October, 2012, 86,590 more registered Democrats in the district than Republicans, and Democratic Party activists held out hope that the *right* candidate could bring back some of these voters to their original home.

The candidate the Democratic Party chose was Gwen Graham, daughter of former Governor and US Senator, Bob Graham, who had retired from the Senate in 2004. Graham had grown up in Tallahassee when her father had been governor and had been an attorney for the Leon County School district for most of her career. She quickly adopted the campaign slogan, "the North Florida Way" to signify her identity with the unique set of values and way of life in Florida's panhandle, an area that is viewed as culturally and politically different from the remainder of the state. She claimed to be a "different type of representative" who wanted to find common ground with Republicans (Campaign announcement, April 2, 2013).

The organizations of both parties, Democrat and Republican, came to the defense of their candidates and both campaigns raised substantial funds. Graham raised $3.6 million and was one of only ten non-incumbents in the nation to raise more money than an incumbent in a congressional race (Clozel 2104), Southerland raised $2.9 million and outside groups spent about $8.5 million on television ads for the two candidates. In addition, Graham organized an unusually large and aggressive *ground game* that included a number of field directors and a hired canvassing staff that worked over 1,500 shifts (Information from Internal campaign documents).

In the end, Graham won the three Democratic counties in the eastern part of the district (Leon, Gadsden, and Jefferson), Southerland won the remaining nine counties, but Graham won a larger share of the vote in all of these counties than did the 2010 candidate and she emerged the winner by 1.2%, 126,096 votes to 123,262 votes. She was one of only two Democratic congressional candidates in the nation to defeat an incumbent Republican (for a more complete analysis of this race, see Crew, Cockerham, and James. forthcoming 2017).

District 3

District 3 includes nine complete counties and parts of three others located on the northeast coast of Florida. It is rated by *Cooks Political Report* as Solid Republican (R+14).

In 2012, Ted Yoho, a Tea Party horse veterinarian who had once suggested that voting be restricted to property owners, took advantage when the district was changed dramatically in the 2011 redistricting and brought four challengers to the race. In the primary, he upset the long time incumbent Cliff Stearns in the Republican primary by about 800 votes. He went on to win the district 3 general election in a heavily Republican district by a 65% to 32% vote against his Democratic opponent.

In 2014, Mr. Yoho sought re-election after becoming one of the most conservative members of the 112th US Congress. Mr. Yoho was one of sixteen House members of the "Conservative Fight Club," a designation meant to describe the "gold standard" for conservatives in the House. As outlined in *RedState*, these members were the sixteen Republicans who voted against the continuing appropriation that would have avoided the impending government shutdown in August 2014 (RedState 2014). Mr. Yoho was also a member of the Congressional Second Amendment Caucus and supported Representative Steve Stockman's (R-Texas) "birther" legislation that would have launched an investigation into President Obama's birth certificate

Mr. Yoho easily turned back a mild challenge in the Republican primary from Jake Rush, a Gainesville attorney and former Alachua County Deputy Sheriff, and went on to defeat Democrat Marihelen Wheeler by 32.7% of the vote in the general election.

District 4

District 4 is located in northeast Florida and includes part of Duval County and all of both Baker and Nassau counties. It is rated a solid Republican seat by *Cook's Political Report* and has been represented since 2000 by

Jacksonville native Ander Crenshaw, a banker. Before coming to Congress, Crenshaw served fourteen years in the Florida State Legislature and was the first Republican Florida Senate president in 118 years.

US Representative Crenshaw is, in its contemporary definition, a relatively moderate Republican who had a 0.62 conservative ranking on the *GovTrack* rating scale. This scale, which is based on votes in US Congress and on public statements about public policy, ranges from 1.0 as the most conservative to 0 as the most liberal. The most liberal Republican in the US House in 2014 achieved a 0.54 score, only slightly more liberal than Crenshaw (GovTrack 2017).

In 2014 Representative Crenshaw faced minimal opposition in his district, but did draw a Republican primary opponent. In that race he defeated, Ryman Shoaf by 70.9% to 29.1% of the vote and went on to win the general election (with 78% of the vote) against two candidates who ran with no party label and one write in.

District 5

US Congressional district 5 snakes like a meandering stream through eight counties in east central Florida, beginning in Duval County (Jacksonville) in the north and ending in Orange County (Orlando) in the south. It was created as a "majority minority" district to satisfy requirements in US Civil Rights law. . Duval and Orange counties comprise about 80% of the population in the district, it is about 52% African American and has a D+18 rating on the Cook's Partisan Voting Index. Democrat Representative Corrine Brown, one of the first three African Americans to represent Florida in Congress in over one hundred years, was first elected to this office in 1993 and has held the seat since that time, despite early attempts by Republicans to replace her.

Despite Brown's seniority and visibility in the district, in 2012 two Republicans, Thuy Lowe and Gloreatha Scurry-Smith, thought they could defeat her and fought in a primary for the right to try. Scurry-Smith was victorious in the primary, but found that she had miscalculated. Brown was re-elected by 30.9% of the vote, 118,559 to 53,108.

District 6

This district is made up of all of Flagler and St. Johns counties as well as portions of Putnam and Volusia counties. In 2014 it had 204,581 registered Republicans and 167,790 registered Democrats and received a R+6 rating on the Cook's PVI. The incumbent in the district was Tea Party backed Republican Ron DeSantis who had emerged from a contested Republican primary to win the seat in 2012 by a substantial margin. His opponent was first time candidate David Cox, director of freshman college resources at Bethune-Cookman University in Daytona Beach. DeSantis raised $1,110,622 and easily vanquished Cox, winning 62.5% of the vote. Cox raised $38,749 (All money totals in this chapter come from Open Secrets).

District 7

Located near the center of Florida, US Congressional district 7 is made up of almost all of Orange County and smaller parts of Seminole and Volusia counties. Republicans have a 41,000 voter registration edge in the district and it has a Cook's PVI of R+5. The incumbent in the office was Republican John Mica who had been in the Congress, although in a different district, since 1992.

Mica's opponents in the campaign were a 32 year old first time Democratic candidate named Wes Neuman from Longwood, Florida. and Independent candidate Al Krulick, a former actor at Disney. In previous years, Krulick had run as a candidate for both the Green Party and as a Democrat. Neuman had a background in public and foreign affairs, largely in Washington, DC (Powers 2014a). Given the nature of the district, both Krulick and Neuman were long shots who no one expected to win. Compounding his low visibility problem, Neuman disappeared from the campaign trail starting in September and was not seen for weeks, leading Krulick to suggest that Democrats should vote for him (Powers 2014a).

In the end, Mica raised $851, 622 in campaign funds, Neuman raised $52,481, and Krulick raised $15,949. Mica won the race by a 31.5% margin.

District 8

In 2014, US Congressional district 8 stretched along Florida's east coast and was made up of Broward, Indian River, and a small portion of Orange counties. It includes the Kennedy Space Center. In 2014, registered Republican voters outpaced registered Democrats by 50,000 individuals and the district had a PVI of R+8. The Republican incumbent, Bill Posey, had been elected to Congress in 2008 after serving sixteen years in the Florida state legislature. In the year before his re-election bid he was ranked as the 107th most conservative member of Congress by the *National Journal*, a conservative political magazine.

His Democratic opponent was Gabriel Rothblatt, a property manager and an insurance broker, who was the son of the founder of both Sirius

Satellite Radio and the pharmaceutical company United Therapeutics and who claimed to be the most highly paid woman CEO in the nation (Siegelbaum 2014).

Both candidates argued in favor of support for the nation's space program and for investment in the space industry. However, the campaign was no contest. Given the nature of the district and the mismatch in candidate qualifications, the Democratic candidate was only able to raise one tenth of the money that was generated on behalf of his opponent ($110 thousand to $1.3 million) and Posey was re-elected by a 31.7% vote margin.

District 9

District 9 includes part of Orange County, and all of rural Polk and Osceola counties. It is very racially diverse with 44.1% Hispanic, 11.8% African American, and 39.5% white residents. The Democrats had a voter registration advantage of about 70,000 votes in the district and it carried a Cook's PVI of D+9.

In 2014, district 9 was represented by Alan Grayson, an outspoken liberal who had called a previous opponent, Daniel Webster, "Taliban Dan," because of what Grayson said were the opponent's "13th century views on women" (Sharockman 2010).

Independently wealthy from his work in telecommunications, Grayson had first won election in district 8, had been defeated there by Mr. Webster, had regained his position in 2102 in the new district 9, and was running for re-election for the first time in his new district.

In spite of the partisan makeup of the district and his own visibility, Grayson found opposition in both his own primary and that of the Republicans, who had three candidates in their race. The Republican winner and Grayson's opponent in the general election was Carol Platt, a real estate agent and rancher who had worked for decades in the area to support agriculture, education, and Republican political campaigns.

The campaign centered around Grayson's persona. Platt accused him of being divisive, calling his words and actions "disgraceful" and contributing to congressional gridlock. Grayson said that Platt was divisive because of her opposition to anything and everything proposed by President Obama (Powers 2014c) This attitude prevented any progress on issues important to the district, he said.

Although Platt raised a respectable $441,127 campaign bank account, Grayson swamped her by accumulating $3.1 million and defeated her by over 10% of the vote.

District 10

District 10 is located in the very center of Florida and cuts across Lake, Polk, and Orange counties. It is heavily Republican (Cook's PVI of R+6) and was represented in 2014 by Daniel Webster, a veteran legislator who had served in the Florida State Legislature for twenty-eight years, including stints as the first Republican Speaker of the House and as Senate president, before being elected to the Congress in 2008.

Despite this unforgiving landscape for a Democrat, three relatively strong candidates emerged in that Party's primary: former Eustis City Commissioner Bill Ferree, pilot Michael McKenna, and Shayan Modarres, a lawyer who had represented the Trayvon Martin family in the highly publicized "stand your ground" case involving Trayvon and the person who killed him, George Zimmerman.

Given their higher name recognition, political pundits rated the race a toss-up between Modarres and Ferree. Nevertheless, McKenna mounted an aggressive campaign, knocked, so he claimed, on 56,000 doors and garnered 49.7% of the votes to emerge the winner.

In the general election, McKenna claimed that Webster had become too comfortable in office and lacked any urgency in representing the district. Webster countered by claiming success in gaining resources for a number of Florida-based projects and by opposing President Obama's signature legislative accomplishment, the *Affordable Care Act* (Powers 2014b; U.S. Congress 2010).

Hugely overmatching his rival financially—Webster raised $1 million to $33,558 for McKenna—Webster went on the win by 23% of the vote; 143,128 to 89,426.

District 11

Florida's Congressional district 11 stretches from Tampa north to five other counties: Sumter, Citrus, Hernando, Marion, and Lake. Heavily Republican in voter registration, it carried a Cook's PVI of R+11. In 2014 it was represented by Richard Nugent, a third term incumbent who had won his 2012 election with 65% of the vote.

Despite this circumstance, Democrat David Koller, an Ocala businessman, stepped forward as a challenger. Koller said he ran because of his frustration with the partisan gridlock in national politics. He described himself as a social progressive and a fiscal conservative. He criticized Nugent for his conservative voting record and for his vote on the debt ceiling and the budget (Pipsorcle 2013).

Nugent admitted that he was a conservative but said that he had worked with a number of Democrats on issues of mental health, veteran's health, and on tax fraud (Pipsorcle 2013).

The outcome of this race was determined when the district lines were drawn and Nugent's three to one advantage in campaign funds—$330,971 to $74,636—ensured his victory. He won by 33.3% of the vote.

District 12

This district is located on the western coast of Florida and is composed of all or part of three counties: Pasco, Hillsborough, and Pinellas. It is a heavily Republican district (Cook's PVI of R+7). Since 1982, the district and its previous incarnations have been represented by Michael and Gus Bilirakis, father and son. When his father retired in 2006, Gus stepped into the seat and has represented it since, even though its borders have been redrawn.

The seat is, like many in Florida, very uncompetitive and in 2014, Bilirakis ran unopposed. Nevertheless, he spent in excess of $700,000 dollars on the campaign.

District 13

District 13 is located on Florida's west coast in Pinellas County and covers the area from Dunedin to St. Petersburg. It is a highly competitive district, carrying a Cook's PVI of R+1 and displaying relatively close voter registration numbers: Republicans, 171,118; Democrats 158,938; and NPA 116,868.

For forty-three years, until October, 2013, the district (and its forerunners) had been represented by Republican Bill Young, the longest serving Republican in the US Congress, who had used his position as Chair of the House Appropriations Committee to deliver millions of federal dollars to his district and Florida's defense industry. On October 18, Congressman Young passed away, setting up a special election to replace him.

Young's death threw both Republicans and Democrats into a search for candidates to contest the seat. The Democrats quickly cleared the field for former Florida Chief Financial Officer and 2010 Democratic candidate for Governor, Alex Sink. Sink had lost the closest race for governor in modern Florida political history under the onslaught of a $70 million campaign that was personally funded by Republican Rick Scott and who had been considering the seat since Young announced that he would retire at the end of his current term. Sink lived just outside the district in adjoining Hillsborough County and said she would move from there into the district (Smith 2013).

The Republicans, on the other hand, endured a long contest that was filled with turmoil and drama between lobbyist David Jolly, a long time Young staffer who had left the staff in 2012 to join the Washington lobby corps, and State Representative Kathleen Peters, who represented southern Pinellas County (Redington Shores to St. Pete Beach) in Florida House district 69.

Within three weeks of Young's death, David Jolly announced plans to succeed his former employer. At his kickoff event, Young's widow, Beverly, endorsed his candidacy and said that her late husband told her on his deathbed that he wanted Jolly to run for his seat. Additional endorsements followed: from US Senator Marco Rubio, "Price is Right" gameshow host Bob Barker, the NRA, former St. Petersburg Mayor Rich Baker, and Florida State Senator Jack Latvala (Jaffe 2014).

Shortly after this announcement, Young's son, Bill, Jr., announced that he was backing Peters, incurring the wrath of his mother, who said "you have hurt me beyond belief" (Jaffe 2014). Then almost immediately the *Tampa Bay Times* published a salacious story about a family that Congressman Young had begun in his youth, abandoned and subsequently kept secret after fathering a son with and then marrying, his former secretary Beverly Angello (Young) (Meacham 2014). The story threatened to tar Young's legacy and Jolly supporters feared it would rub off on their candidate.

As the primary got underway, some analysts saw Peters as the better candidate since she did not carry the lobbyist baggage that the Democrats were tying around Jolly's neck and could perhaps neutralize any attacks that focused on women's issues. In the end, she simply could not raise enough money to be a serious candidate. Jolly raised more than twice the amount that Peters was able to generate and easily dispatched her by 45% to 31% of the vote with a third candidate Mark Binder, receiving 24% of the vote.

When the general election began, there was substantial optimism in the Democratic camp. The district had been moving in that Party's direction for a number of years. President Obama had won it two cycles in a row and Sink defeated Rick Scott there in 2010 with 51.5 % of the vote. Her name recognition was high and she had the ability to raise a lot of money. She made a point of appealing to independent voters and hoped to turn out the Democratic base and peel off some Republican moderates.

On the other hand, the district was made up almost entirely of white voters, there was a slight Republican voter registration advantage, and it had long tilted conservative. Jolly appealed to this constituency by tying himself as closely as possible to Bill Young, by making opposition to the *Affordable Care Act* the centerpiece of his campaign, and by taking conservative positions on most other issues. He opposed immigration reform and gun control and believed *Roe v. Wade* should be overturned.

The race was one of the most expensive special elections in Florida history. The Sink campaign was especially effective, outperforming the Jolly organization by generating $1.6 million to $858,000 for Jolly (Fox 2014). Both the Republican and the Democratic Parties also bet big on the race. "National Republican groups ... combined to spend nearly $5 million, much of it on tying Sink to President Obama's unpopular Affordable Care Act. Democrats, meanwhile, poured in nearly $4 million, and used it to portray Jolly as a cold-hearted opponent of entitlement programs and abortion rights" (Isenstadt 2014).

Despite the attention brought to the race by national news coverage, turnout was very low (the general election turnout in previous elections, even in a safe seat for Bill Young, had been nearly twice as high) and on March 3, Jolly defeated Sink by 3,417 votes out of the 182,103 cast for four candidates. The Republicans attributed their victory to popular dissatisfaction with Obamacare, and lauded it as a positive sign for the upcoming midterm elections around the nation (Isenstadt 2014).

In the decidedly anti-climatic general election held in November, Sink decided against making a second attempt at the seat. The Democrats nominated Lucas Overby who raised $55,603 to counteract the $2 million generated by the Jolly campaign and Jolly was re-elected by a margin of 75.2% to 24.7% of the vote.

District 14

This district is composed of 10% of Pinellas County and half of Hillsborough County, is located in the western half of the state, and is dominated by the City of Tampa. It is a racially diverse district with a strong Democratic lean (D+13 on Cook's PVI), and has been in the hands of Democrat Kathy Castor since 2006. Castor is moderately liberal, carrying a 0.31 rating on *GovTrack*'s ideology scale, where 1.00 is most conservative and 0 is most liberal. She ranks as the 373rd most conservative member of Congress (GovTrack 2017) Although the Republicans ran a candidate against Castor in 2012, they gave up in 2014, leaving her to run unopposed.

District 15

A solid Republican district with a Cook's PVI of R+6, district 15 is located in Hillsborough and Polk counties and is racially very homogenous. Although registered voters are relatively equal (40.0% Republican, 39.1% Democrat, and 20.8% unaffiliated), the district was very conservative and had been won by Republican Dennis Ross in 2010 when longtime incumbent Adam Putnam left to run for the state's Commissioner of Agriculture and Consumer Services position. Ross had served in the Florida House of Representatives for eight years and in 2012 was ranked by the *National Journal* as the 15th most conservative member of Congress (National Journal 2017). He ran unopposed in 2012, but drew opposition from Democrat Alan Cohn in 2014. Cohn, an investigative news reporter at WFTS-Channel 28 in Tampa, had won a Peabody Journalism Award in 2007, and claimed that his background in local TV news gave him an advantage in name recognition (March 2014).

Cohn attacked Ross for opposing the vote to reauthorize the *Violence Against Women Act of 1994 (VAWA)*, and said that Ross was one of the most anti-middle class, anti-woman members of Congress. She said, "He's opposed to equal pay, marriage equality, a living wage, and immigration reform" (DownWithTyranny 2014).

In his brief tenure in Congress, Ross had stuck with his Tea Party supported free-market principles on fiscal matters and was recognized by the National Taxpayers Union and other conservative groups. He had also moved into GOP leadership circles by attaching himself to Representative Steve Scalise who became the Republican Party Whip in the aftermath of Majority Leader Eric Cantor's upset election loss.

Although early polls showed some support for Cohn, he had little chance against a conservative opponent in a conservative district who had access to substantial sums of money. In the end, Ross raised nearly times the money as did Cohn ($1.2 million to $444,000) and went on to win by a 20% margin, 128,750 to 84,832.

District 16

Composed of part of Manatee and all of Sarasota counties, district 16 is a strong Republican district with a Cook's PVI of R+6 and a Republican registered voter advantage of 206,864 to 112,178 for the Democrats. Since 2010 it had been represented by Alan Cohn, a member of the important Ways and Means Committee who, according to the *National Journal* ranked in the top half of the most conservative legislators in Congress (National Journal 2017)

As an incumbent in 2014, Vern Buchanan drew no opposition in the primary and the Democrats endorsed, but put no resources into the campaign of Henry Lawrence, a former lineman in the National Football League. Lawrence himself raised about $63,000 ($11,000 from his own pocket) and, by the end of June, had only $173 in the bank. Buchanan, on the other hand, raised $1.6 million and basically ignored Lawrence in the campaign. He won re-election by a 23% voter margin.

District 17

Another safe district, in 2014, Congressional district 17 was a highly Republican (Cooke's PVI of R+11) district located in the middle of the state and composed of all or parts of ten counties. It was home to Tom Rooney who had been a member of Congress since 2008 and who was related to the owners of the Pittsburg Steelers NFL team. Rooney himself had been a reliably conservative member of Congress and was rated 55th on the *National Journal*'s ranking of conservatives in the US House (National Journal 2017).

In the campaign, Rooney opposed Obamacare, and called for an overhaul of the tax code and for "pro-growth, pro-job" policies (Tampa Bay times 2014b). He raised nearly $600,000 to run against Bill Bronson, a retired airline pilot who he had defeated in 2012 by 17.2% of the vote. Bronson supported the *Dream Act* and pushed for an expansion of Medicare. Bronson, who had once run for Congress as a Republican, raised only $22,000. In an easy victory in 2014, the electoral differences between the two candidates was increased to 26.4% of the vote, with Rooney winning by 141,493 to 82,263.

District 18

In 2012, this district had been the site of one of the most visible congressional elections in the United States as the Democrats mobilized in a newly created district to combat an aggressive, hostile Tea Party star, Allen West, who had spent his first term in Congress sending out thunderbolt proclamations such as "[President Obama is] probably the dumbest person walking around in America right now" (Isenstadt 2012). Despite a war chest of $19 million, West had been defeated by 0.6% of the vote by Patrick Murphy and Republicans were anxious to challenge him in 2014,

In 2014, district 18 was composed of 300 precincts scattered over Martin, St. Lucie, and Palm Beach counties. It leaned Republican (Cook's PVI of R+3) and contained 37% registered Republicans, 35.3% Democrats, and 23% unaffiliated. The incumbent in the district, Murphy, had converted from a Republican in 2011 to become a moderate Democrat in his first session in Congress and was ranked the 9th most conservative Democrat in the House by the *National Journal* (2017).

Hoping to win back a marginal Republican seat, that party conducted a primary that drew five candidates and nominated Carl Domino, an investment manager who had been a member of the Florida House of Representatives between 2002 and 2010.

In the general election Domino positioned himself as a fiscal conservative who also believed that there was a place for limited government. "I understand that government has a role in doing some things," he said. He opposed the *Affordable Care Act*, wanted to lower business taxes, and to "get rid of a lot of unnecessary regulations." Further, while he personally opposed abortion, he accepted the US Supreme Court's position on the issue (Bukley 2014). Domino also tried to portray Murphy as a lackey for the Democrats and ran television ads claiming he voted with Democrat Speaker of the House Nancy Pelosi 84% of the time during his first term (Derby 2014a).

Murphy played up his moderation and his independence. He supported the *Affordable Care Act* but called for adjustments to it and supported a pathway to citizenship for people who were in the United States illegally—if they learned English, paid back taxes, and "got to the back of the line" (Bennet 2014). He released ads that featured support from independent and Republican voters praising him and others featured an article from a national conservative publication that classified him in the top 5% of the most independent members of the Congress (Greenberg 2015) He also was one of only six congressional Democrats who was endorsed by the US Chamber of Commerce (Bennet 2014). Further enhancing his moderate, bi-partisan image, he also refrained from attacking his opponent personally.

Domino was a serious candidate who ran a strong campaign supported by $1.5 million in contributions, of which $485,000 came from his own sources. Nevertheless, he was no match for Murphy, who was the top Democratic fundraiser in the House, collecting more than $4.3 million.

When the campaign ended, Murphy won 59.8% of the vote and established himself as a major player in the Democratic Party of Florida.

District 19

In 2012, the election in this heavily Republican district (Cook's PVI of R+11) became the site of a free-for-all Republican primary when the previous incumbent, Connie Mack IV, resigned to run for the US Senate. The victor in this five candidate primary was a political newcomer and former conservative talk show host Trey Radel. A Tea Party candidate, Radel went on to win the general election by 27% points.

A "hard-edged, ... libertarian-leaning Republican" (Caputo 2013), Radel was one of the first group of Republicans in the Congress to begin talk regarding a federal government shutdown and suggested impeaching President Obama over gun use. In addition "Radel made a splash in D.C. by appearing to be a younger, hipper version of fellow Florida Republican and rap lover, Sen. Marco Rubio." (Caputo 2013)

He made an even bigger splash ten months into his term in October, 2013, when, after voting for drug testing for food stamp recipients, he was busted for possession of cocaine (Caputo 2013). In the aftermath of the charge and after pressure from a variety of Republican officials, including drug testing supporter Governor Rick Scott, Radel resigned his congressional seat, setting up a special election called by Scott for April with the general election to be held in June of 2014.

As a safe Republican district, the April race drew a large field to the Republican primary. They included Florida Senate Majority Leader Lizbeth Benacquisto, State Representative Paige Kreegel, who had run for the seat in 2012, and two businessmen Michael Dreikorn and former Purdue University basketball player, Curt Clawson, who was the CEO of an aluminum wheel company. The race also drew a large number of GOP heavyweight supporters, such as Sara Palin, Senator Rand Paul, and the seat's previous occupant, Connie Mack IV, who had been the Republican Party candidate for the US Senate in 2012.

Given the issue similarities among the candidates, the race degenerated into a "decidedly negative affair, with hyperbolic accusations and character assassination floated freely in television ads, mailers and news stories bombarding Southwest Florida voters" (King. 2014). Clawson injected almost $3 million of his own money into the race, cast himself as a political outsider who would cut taxes, reduce the deficit, and repeal the *Affordable Care Act*, and he jumped out to an early lead in the polls (Montanaro, Burlij, Wellford, and Pathe 2014). His opponents banded together to attack him and made separate charges against each other (Hwysocki@newspress.com 2014). Nevertheless, with the support of Rand Paul and the Tea Party, Clawson collected over a third of the total votes and won by 38% to 26% for Benacquisto 25% for Kreegel, and 11% for Dreikorn.

In the general election held in June, Clawson easily defeated Democrat April Freeman by 67% to 30%, with 3% going to a Libertarian candidate.

District 20

This district is one of Florida's *minority majority* districts created to ensure that minority segments of the population can effectively compete for public office in the state. It was made up of three counties, Broward, Hendry, and Palm Beach, and had an overwhelmingly Democratic voter advantage: 248,659 Democrat, 47,982 Republican, and 78,675 unaffiliated. It also carried a massive Democratic edge in the Cook rating scheme (PVI of D+29) as the 4th most Democratic district in the nation.

The incumbent in the district was Alcee Hastings, who had held his seat in Congress since 1992 and who had been Florida's first African American appointee to the federal bench. A fixture in the Democratic Party and in Congress, Hastings was not challenged in the Democratic primary, raised $710 thousand to his Republican opponent's $30,000 in the general election, and defeated Jay Bonner by 81.6% of the vote to 18.4%. An additional non-competitive race in Florida.

District 21

Another of Florida's non-competitive congressional districts, district 21 is located in Palm Beach and Broward counties, and is ranked D+10 on Cook's PVI scale. In a special election held in 2010 to fill a seat vacated by Robert Wexler, Ted Deutch, an attorney and former Florida state senator, defeated a Republican and an unaffiliated candidate by 62% to 36% of the vote. In 2012, he ran against two unaffiliated candidates and again won an overwhelming victory. Again in 2014, the Republicans recognized the futility of supporting a candidate in the district; Deutch raised over $1 million to defeat Independent Mike Trout by 153,395 votes to 575.

District 22

Over a ten year period between 2004 and 2014, the counties in this district (Broward and Palm Beach) experienced the election of four different members of Congress, alternating in each of four elections between Democrats and Republicans. In 2004, longtime incumbent Republican Clay Shaw was defeated by Democrat Ron Klein, who served two terms before losing to Tea Party zealot Alan West in 2010, who was subsequently replaced in 2012 by Democrat Lois Frankel when West moved to another district after reapportionment, and was subsequently ousted from Congress.

In the period described above, the district had gradually become more Democratic. In 2012, 54% of its voters cast ballots for President Obama and in 2014 and it carried a Cook's PVI of D+3,

In 2014, incumbent Frankel had held public office for twenty six of the previous twenty-eight years. She had been a member of the Florida House of Representatives between 1986 and 1992, a member of the state Senate between 1994 and 2002, and the Mayor of the City of Palm Peach from 2003 to 2011.

Although an avowed liberal, Frankel had worked with both Republicans and Democrats in Congress and in the legislature, and argued that a low seniority member could accomplish goals "if you keep your head down and know how to maneuver in the process" (Gibson 2014a). She supported the

Affordable Care Act but suggested it could use amendments and promised to "crack down on Medicare fraud" (Gibson 2014a).

Given the district's volatility in the previous ten years, Republicans in 2014 still thought a victory there was within grasp and three candidates showed up in the Party's primary, which was won by Paul Spain, a retired banker and financial planner from Delray Beach, Florida.

As the general election began, the Republican began to recognize his limitations. First, district demographics had moved steadily toward the Democrats who had a 40.1% to 31.1% voter registration advantage. Secondly, Frankel generated a substantial financial advantage and raised $1.3 million while Spain, who put $83,000 of his own money into his effort, was able to raise only about $60,000 from other sources, giving him a total of $145,367.

Spain made the usual Republican promises to: help businesses thrive, create jobs, and spur the economy by cutting taxes and federal spending, but when the election closed Frankel won 125,404 votes to 90,685 votes for Spain, and 7 votes to write-in candidate Raymond Schamis, thus solidifying the Democratic Party's position in this swing district.

District 23

District 23 is one of the most Democratic and most liberal districts in Florida. Carrying a Cook's PVI of D+9, voters in the district have supported the Democratic candidate for President in every election since 2000, and the smallest percentage of the Democratic vote over this period was 62%. The district consists of a major part of Broward County and some of Palm Beach County. It includes the cities of Weston, Plantation, Hollywood, Davie, and Miami Beach.

The district has a very large Jewish population and has been represented since 2004 by Debbie Wasserman Schultz, who is the Chair of the Democratic National Committee. An outspoken liberal, Wasserman Schultz has engendered a high level of animosity among her detractors and she is "arguably one of the most hated woman [*sic*] in politics today" (Manjarres 2014).

As their candidate in 2014, the Republicans nominated "Crazy Joe" Kaufman, a writer/researcher/lecturer who had been a candidate for the Florida House in both 1998 and 2000 and for Congress in 2012. Endorsed by Herman Cain, Newt Gingrich, Rick Santorum, and numerous other conservative leaders, Kaufman's supporters claimed that Wasserman Schultz had prioritized the Democrats' national liberal agenda over her own district and he wanted to "banish the current tax code'" and replace Obamacare with state run insurance pools (Gibson 2014c). Despite their heated rhetoric, Republicans are at a distinct disadvantage in the district and Wasserman Schultz is an excellent candidate who never takes re-election for granted. She raised $2.5 million in campaign funds, was highly active throughout the campaign and won the election by 62.7% to 37.3% of the vote.

District 24

Florida's 24th Congressional district is located primarily in Miami-Dade County with 18% located in Broward County. It is another of Florida's *minority majority* districts. A very strong Democratic county, it carries the highest score in Florida on Cook's PVI of D+34, and has the 7th highest such score in the nation. In 2014, there were 253,228 registered Democrats in the district and only 37,744 registered Republicans,

Given these characteristics, the battle for the congressional seat comes within the Democratic Party, with Republicans rarely fielding a candidate. From 1992 until 2012, the seat, in various incarnations as redistricting took place, had been held by the Meek family, mother and son. In that year, Kendrick Meek resigned to run for the US Senate, sparking an energetic battle between five candidates in the Democratic Party primary and subsequently in the general election between an African American female, Frederica Wilson, and a Haitian male, Rudolph Moise.

Wilson, a long-time member of the Florida state legislature who was well-known for her extravagant hats, emerged as the winner and ran for re-election in 2014 against a very weak Republican candidate and two Independents, Luis Fernandez and Alejandro Walters. Wilson claimed that she didn't even know her GOP opponent's name, which was Dufirston Neree (Gibson 2014b). Neree was an international and community development expert who had run for Congress before but had little political experience and raised only $12, 040 in campaign funds.

Wilson raised over $500,000 and pushed for passage of a jobs bill that would provide tax incentives to hire the unemployed. She won 86.2% of the vote and defeated Neree by 129,192 votes to 15,239 votes.

District 25

This district stretches across the state of Florida from the Gulf of Mexico to the Atlantic Ocean and includes all or part of four counties: Broward, Collier, Hendry, and Miami-Dade. The incumbent in the district, Mario Diaz-Balart, has been in Congress for sixteen years, is known for being a budget hawk and for supporting minority rights. His position in the district was so strong in 2012 that the Democrats could come up with an opponent only by drafting an 87 year old ex-Communist who had been brought before the House

Un-American Affairs Committee in the 1960's. In 2014, they could not find a candidate with even these credentials and Diaz-Balart ran unopposed, one of only four congressional candidates in Florida in 2014 to do so.

District 26

District 26 includes parts of Monroe and Miami-Dade counties and was one of two additional districts awarded to Florida as a result of the state's population gain reported in the 2010 US Census. It is heavily Hispanic but its traditional Cuban base has recently enlarged to encompass Nicaraguans, Columbians, Dominicans, and Venezuelans. It is a very competitive district that leans Republican and has a Cook's PVI of R+1, but elected a Democrat, Joe Garcia in 2012 after the incumbent Republican David Rivera was charged with violating multiple ethics laws (Mazzel and Sherman 2012)

In the ensuing two years, Garcia himself came under ethics charges related to elections violations for which his chief of staff had been convicted during Garcia's unsuccessful 2010 campaign, and he was considered one of the most vulnerable Democratic incumbents in the nation. Republicans sensed an opening and five candidates entered the Party's primary. Carlos Curbelo, a small business owner and a member of the Miami-Dade County school board, emerged the winner with 47% of the vote.

During the general election campaign, Curbelo focused on the charges against Garcia claiming "for far too long, scandal has plagued this district and made it impossible to advance meaningful solutions in Congress to move or community, state and entire country forward" (Derby 2014b).

Although Garcia had earned local bipartisan support and tackled national issues like immigration, the claims made by Curbelo and the Republicans were hard to defend, especially given the gap in campaign funds between the two candidates. Republican outside groups poured more than $6 million into Curbelo's race and his own campaign raised about $2 million. This was in contrast to the $5.5 million total generated by the Democrats and the Garcia campaign. Curbelo won by 52% to 48% of the vote.

District 27

The second of Florida's new Congressional districts was contained in Miami-Dade and Monroe counties, district 27 was 67% Hispanic and carried a Cook's PVI of R+2, even though there were more registered Democrats in the district than Republicans.

The incumbent was Republican Ilena Ros-Lehtinen who had been first elected in a special election in 1989 to replace legendary Democrat Claude

Pepper, who had represented Florida in Congress for over forty-one years, fifteen in the US Senate and twenty-six in this seat in the House of Representatives. Carrying Pepper's longevity forward to 2014, Ros-Lehtinen was the senior female Republican in the US House of Representatives, the first Republican woman elected to Congress from Florida, and the first Latina ever elected to Congress.

Ros-Lehtinen is a political moderate. She is 12th from the bottom among Republicans ranked on the *National Journal*'s conservative rating scale, and many political consultants think she is the only Republican who can survive in her district, which voted for Barack Obama in both 2008 and 2012. No one was willing to challenge her in 2014 and she was one of the four congressional candidates in Florida to run unopposed.

THE PATTERN OF OUTCOMES IN THE 2012 CONGRESSIONAL ELECTIONS

In the 2014 congressional elections in Florida, candidates ran in districts that had been declared unconstitutionally biased toward Republicans and that had been ordered redrawn. However, the ruling on this issue came too close to the time that the 2014 elections were to be held and reapportionment was put off until a later time. In the paragraphs to follow, we examine the patterns in these outcomes and compare them to those in 2012.

Party Success

Both the Democrats and the Republicans maintained their numbers in Congress in the aftermath of the 2014 election. Although the death of Representative Bill Young in district 13 and his replacement by David Jolly resulted in one new face in the delegation, neither party lost a seat and the Republicans maintained their seventeen to ten lead in membership. The Republican majority in the Florida congressional delegation has now been sustained since 1990, or thirteen congressional cycles.

Incumbency Success

Congressional elections in Florida are traditionally won by incumbents, although the incumbency success rate is somewhat lower in the state than in others. After reapportionment in 2012, eight incumbents were replaced, four by losses to a challenger from the opposing party and four who were

Table 6.1. Congressional Incumbency Electoral Success, Florida and the Nation (1982–2014)

	Percent of Incumbents Re-elected	
Year	Florida[1]	Nation[2]
1982	100%	90%
1984	100%	95%
1986	100%	98%
1988	94%	98%
1990	94%	96%
1992	100%	88%
1994	100%	90%
1996	100%	94%
1998	100%	98%
2000	100%	98%
2002	95%	96%
2004	100%	98%
2006	95%	94%
2008	88%	94%
2010	83%	85%
2012	68%	90%
2014	96%	95%

Sources: For the percentage of incumbents re-elected in Florida (1) see Open Secrets, 2017, "Election Overview," *Open Secrets.org*. http://www.opensecrets.org/overview/reelect.php; and for the Nation (2) see Wikipedia, 2017, "United States Congressional Delegations from Florida," https://en.wikipedia.org/wiki/United_States_congressional_delegations_from_Florida#2003_.E2.80.93_2013:_25_seats.

replaced by members of their own party in redrawn districts. In combination, these losses pushed the rate of incumbent success to 68%, the lowest in the state's history. However, in 2014 the "low" rate in 2012 rebounded to a level not seen since 2004 and only one incumbent (Bill Young who passed away) failed to reclaim their seat. That is the incumbency success rate in 2104 was 96%. Table 6.1 displays these rates over the period 1982-2014.

Losses/Gains by the Party of the President

Absent the attention generated by a presidential election, off year elections typically result in downticket losses by the party of the president and the party that holds the White House has lost strength in all but three midterm elections since 1934 (American Presidency Project 2017). In 2014, this phenomenon was continued at the national level and the Democrats lost thirteen congressional seats around the country. In Florida, however, the Party sustained no such losses and all ten Democrats were re-elected.

Electoral Competitiveness

Whether measured by registered voters or by partisan identification, the Florida electorate is evenly divided and Presidential elections in Florida are highly competitive. In the four presidential elections held between 2000 and 2012, the average margin of victory in the state was 0.03% of the vote and the largest margin was 5%. Democrats won two of the elections and Republicans won two.

For a variety of reasons, including determined efforts by Republicans to gain advantage through control of the redistricting process, this level of competitiveness is not replicated in congressional elections in Florida. These campaigns draw few contenders and are rarely very competitive. Over the period 1982-2012, more than two thirds (67%) of Florida congressional elections were *safe* for one of the two major parties; that is, they were either completely unopposed, included races in which one of the major parties did not field a candidate or were decided by margins greater than 21%. At the same time, only seventeen of these races (0.05%) were decided in elections in which the margins were smaller than 5%. These data are shown in table 6.2.

Table 6.2.   Competitiveness in Florida Congressional Elections (1982–2014)

Year	<5%	5-10%	11-20%	21-40%	>40%	Unopposed	Races with No Major Party Opposition
1982	1	1	3	5	6	3	0
1984	0	0	3	6	2	7	1
1986	0	0	0	3	7	7	2
1988	1	2	0	3	5	6	2
1990	2	0	5	4	2	5	1
1992	5	2	7	5	1	2	1
1994	1	1	3	6	1	7	4
1996	1	0	2	13	4	3	0
1998	0	0	1	4	1	15	2
2000	2	0	4	4	5	0	8
2002	1	1	2	8	4	6	3
2004	0	0	1	12	2	5	5
2006	3	1	7	8	0	5	1
2008	1	3	7	9	3	2	0
2010	0	3	4	10	7	1	4
2012	2	3	5	8	3	2	4
2014	1	2	2	12	2	4	4

Source: Calculated by author from data at Florida Department of State, 2017b, *Division of Elections*, http://dos.myflorida.com/elections.

This pattern continued in the elections of 2014. Of the congressional races, 81.4% were *safe*. Four incumbents ran in races where their only opposition came from write in candidates or from non-partisan candidates; four candidates ran completely unopposed; twelve races were decided by margins between 21% and 40%; and two were decided by margins greater than 41%. Only one election (0.03%) was truly competitive and decided by less than 5% of the vote.

According to *FollowTheMoney*'s calculations, Florida ranks 44th of the fifty states in political competitiveness. That is only six states are less politically competitive than Florida (Casey 2016).

The absence of competition in elections creates a variety of problems for democracies. One is that contact between constituents and elected officials decreases. Citizens who share partisan affiliation with the member assume he/she is representing them on the basis of their shared partisanship. Citizens who do not share partisanship assume that the member from the other party will not be amenable to their interests.

Lack of competition also contributes to increased levels of partisanship. When candidates are able to win simply through appeals to members of their own party, they have no incentive to moderate their views on issues of public policy or to move to the center of the ideological spectrum. This phenomenon is endemic in American politics and in Florida.

Chapter Seven

The Campaigns for
the Florida State Legislature

The Florida Senate is composed of forty members, elected to four year terms on a staggered basis. The twenty senators in odd-numbered districts are elected in US presidential election years, while senators in even-numbered districts are elected in midterm election years. All seats are up for re-election in redistricting years, with some terms truncated as a result. In the midterm elections of 2014, the twenty even numbered districts were scheduled for elections. When the election began, the Republicans held twenty-six seats and the Democrats held fourteen. When the election was completed, the numbers remained the same.

THE STATE SENATE CAMPAIGNS

The 2014 elections for the Florida State Senate were characterized by a lack of interest on the part of the public and an exercise in futility for citizens who think of elections as an opportunity to discuss issues of public policy and to choose among candidates who express alternative versions of how to address these issues.

Only ten of the twenty eligible districts generated enough interest to hold a general election at all; the other ten were won by the incumbent without competition. Further, only six Republicans and two Democrats faced opposition in their party's primary. Thus, *40% of the state senators elected in the State of Florida in 2014 were selected when they signed official papers declaring their candidacy.*

Nine of the remaining ten positions were filled with only marginally greater effort. Eight of these were won by margins of 21% of the vote or greater (FairVote's definition of a landslide, See "Dubious Democracy 1994"), and one was determined by a margin of 15.4% of the vote. Only one race was competitive and was decided by a margin of 5% percent or less of the vote. In five of the ten contested districts, there was only one major party candidate running for election. These results are damning to those who create electoral districts in Florida and demoralizing to proponents of democracy.

Following is a description of the single competitive race for state Senate in 2014.

Senate District 34

This district runs along Florida's Atlantic Coast from Boynton Beach to Fort Lauderdale with roughly half of the district in each of two counties, Broward and Palm Beach. Politically, the district leans Democrat with 39.7% registered Democrats, 31.4% Republican, and 25.6% registered unaffiliated (All data regarding voter registration and voting outcomes from Florida Division of Elections). In 2014 the district was represented by Democrat Maria Sachs who had won the seat in 2012 against Republican Ellyn Bogdanoff. The 2014 race was a rerun of that race which was the most closely contested Senate seat in the 2012 electoral cycle.

Maria Sachs is a lawyer who had been an Assistant State Attorney and a member of the Florida House of Representatives prior to being elected to the state Senate in 2010. Her first campaign against Bogdanoff had come as a result of the 2010 redistricting plan that threw the two incumbents into the same district and created the only incumbent vs. incumbent race in that year. Running on the same ticket as President Obama helped immeasurably with Democratic turnout and despite a substantial fundraising deficit, Sachs won by 5.6% of the vote.

In 2014, both Democrats and Republicans thought the President's absence from the ticket would affect the outcome of the race. The first election after a presidential race usually isn't very good for the president's party and Republicans were banking on lukewarm enthusiasm on the part of Democrats to keep turnout low and boost Bogdanoff's chances. Nevertheless, the Democratic tilt in registration figures and her incumbency status gave Sachs a slight edge in pre-election forecasts.

The race was especially important since it represented the difference between Republicans having a super majority and being able to completely ignore the Democrats, versus having only a *normal* majority and being required to pay at least glancing deference to them. If Bogdanoff won, the Republicans would have a super majority.

The first race between the two candidates, in 2012, had been aggressive, expensive, and negative. Both sides spent a lot of money on negative ads directed against the opponent's policy positions and personal behavior. The 2014 race was somewhat less hostile, although Bogdanoff did raise an issue related to Sachs' residence. While the Democrat claimed to live in a Broward condo in her district, videos showed her entering and leaving a Palm Beach County estate not located in her district. Sachs claimed she owned them both and normally slept in the condo "seven nights a week" (Miami Herald 2013).

Moderate for a Republican, Bogdanoff focused on business issues, education, children's issues, and criminal justice. Sachs "worried" about property insurance, education, and the effects of climate change (Sweeney 2014b). Their interests in education policy were divergent: Bogdanoff favored conservative reforms such as vouchers and charter schools, while Sachs called for increased funding for public education and saw increases for charters and vouches as money that would be better spent increasing the quality of traditional public schools (Sweeney 2014b).

Bolstered by support from a range of special interest groups such as the National Federation of Independent Businesses and the Business Action Committee of Palm Beach County, the Bogdanoff campaign, as it had done in the prior election, raised substantially more money than did Sachs (Sweeney 2014b). However, both political parties made this race a high priority and made heavy contributions to their candidates. In the end, Bogdanoff had a $2,843,682 campaign war chest compared to $2,830,881 for Sachs (All information regarding fundraising from Open Secrets website). Both of these numbers are enormous for state legislative races.

Both campaigns spent liberally on both broadcast and cable television and ended up at parity in these media. The Bogdanoff campaign spent a total of $2,062,676 on television compared to $2,037,380 for Sachs (Sachs Campaign internal data. Through personal contacts, the authors had access to the internal reports of several campaigns in the 2014 cycle). This parity was a substantial factor in the Sachs victory. As John Sides and Lynn Vavreck have shown, candidates who have a one GRP (gross rating point) advantage in a market—about one ad per capita more than an opponent—could expect to gain almost an additional point of vote share, compared to a market in which two candidates were at parity in television advertising (Sides and Vavreck 2013, 130). Thus, neither side was advantaged here.

The Sachs campaign also conducted a substantial field campaign that knocked on 71,512 doors and made 71,760 telephone calls (Sachs campaign internal documents).

Despite the absence of Barak Obama on the presidential ticket, a highly competent campaign organization and strategy allowed Sachs to once again defeated Bogdanoff, by 4.2% of the vote, only slightly less than the margin in 2012 .

HOUSE OF REPRESENTATIVES CAMPAIGNS

All 120 seats in the House of Representatives were up for election in 2014. When the campaign began, the Republicans held seventy-four of these seats and the Democrats held forty-six. When it ended, the totals were eighty for the Republicans to forty for the Democrats. Many of the Democratic loses were the product of the voter turnout decline that takes place in all off year elections and that falls more heavily on Democrats than Republicans.

As was the case with the state Senate, competition in the House of Representatives was minimal. In the general election, forty-seven candidates, or 40%, ran completely unopposed and only fourteen incumbents faced primary opposition. In another twenty-two seats, there was only one major party candidate seeking the seat. In combination with the completely unopposed candidates, twenty-eight Democrats and forty-one Republicans were virtually assured victory when they filed for office. *In short, nearly one-half (49.2%) of the 120 candidates elected to the Florida House of Representatives in 2014 achieved their seats simply by filing their election paperwork.*

In contrast, only five districts in the elections were truly competitive, or decided by less than 5% of the vote. These were districts 29, 30, 47, 49, 65 and 112. Five of these seats were won by Republicans and one by a Democrat.

Three of these competitive races involved Central Florida Democrats who, spurred by the large turnout attributed to the presence of Barack Obama on the presidential ticket, won seats in 2012 by defeating incumbent Republicans in competitive seats. When this turnout declined in 2014, these 2012 winners were left vulnerable.

Two other candidates, in districts 29 and 65, succumbed to the "exposure" phenomenon in that each were defending seats that they had picked up in the preceding election in districts dominated by the opposite party and that were not *natural* for their own party.

One other race, in district 112, involved a competitive candidate in a competitive district who lost a well-run campaign.

The distribution of competitiveness in both houses of the legislature is shown in table 7.1.. It shows that in 2014, more than one half (56.4%) of

Table 7.1. Margin of Victory, Florida House, and Senate Elections, 2014

Florida Congress	<5%	5-10%	11-20%	21-40%	>40%	Unopposed
House	5	7	21	16	23	47
Senate	1	0	1	5	3	10

Source: Calculated by author from data at Florida Department of State, 2017b, *Division of Elections,* http://dos.myflorida.com/elections

all the members of the combined Florida State Senate and Florida House of Representatives achieved their positions simply by paying a minimal filing fee. Only seven candidates, or 5%, *of all those elected to the Florida State Legislature in 2014*, were selected in truly competitive campaigns. The citizens of Florida are short changed by this process.

In the following paragraphs, we describe the nature of the campaigns in the five competitive State House districts.

District 30

In 2012, Democrat Karen Castor Dentel rode the Obama turnout machine to victory in what was then a newly created district, formerly held by a Republican, and captured this highly competitive legislative seat against one of the most conservative GOP candidate in the state, Scott Plakon.

Reflecting their sense of ownership of the seat, Republicans began filing to run against Castor Dentel in the 2014 electoral cycle less than three months after her swearing in ceremony in 2012. In a subsequent spirited primary, they selected Bob Cortes, the owner of a tow-truck company who served on the Longwood City Commission from 2009 to 2012 as their candidate.

In contrast to the Republican's ideologically extreme candidate in 2012, Cortes was a relatively moderate, business oriented Republican who ran on a fairly standard program of cutting taxes, reducing regulations on businesses, and, in the education arena, calling for more focus on the classroom and more vocational training (Henderson 2014).

Castor Dentel promoted her support for efforts to improve Florida's economy, to secure funds for infrastructure development, for education funding, and for job training. She ran a series of attack ads that claimed Cortes's support for charter schools and vouchers was tantamount to a "scheme that drains millions from public schools" (Torres 2017).

The Castor Dentel campaign was carried in the field, on television, and by mail. In cooperation with the Orange County Democratic Executive Committee (DEC), the campaign knocked on 39,432 doors with 8,847 contacts. At the same time, the campaign made 19,999 phone calls and contacted 4,319 contacts. The mail program focused on unaffiliated voters and a targeted universe of Republicans that excluded men and primary voting party members. The positive message points in the mail were "local control of Schools," "equal pay for equal work," and "ending tax handouts for special interests." (Castor Dentel internal campaign documents)

The size difference between the two campaigns' television programs likely made the difference in the race. Overall, Cortes outspent Castor Dentel by $589,815 to $295,206 on television, a two to one ratio. Much of this came from the Republican Party of Florida, which made the district a high priority and spent $394,700 on television on her behalf (Florida Center for Public Integrity 2014).

Specifically on broadcast, Castor Dentel was outspent by $589,815 to $157,500, a four to one ratio (Castor Dentel campaign documents). Further, while her cable television program started on September 23rd, Castor Dentel was unable to get up on broadcast television until midweek on October 7th. During weeks five and six, Cortes outspent Castor Dentell by a six to one ratio. These differences gave the Cortes campaign a large advantage in gross rating points and a full week and a half of unanswered air time on broadcast television.

When one candidate is able to air more advertisements than the other, votes will shift. In a presidential race, "other things equal, a candidate who has a 100 GRP advantage in a market could expect to gain almost an additional point of vote share" (Sides and Vavreck 2013, 130). In a downticket race such as this where information about candidates is scarcer, the differences cited above certainly had an even greater impact.

Given these deficiencies, absent the presidential race, and Barack Obama at the head of the ticket, overall voting turnout in the district fell by 30% from the preceding election (Democrats declined by 36%) and Castor Dentel's vote share among non-Cuban Hispanics fell from 71% in 2012 to 47% in 2014 (Castor Dentel internal campaign documents). Cortes pulled out a narrow victory, returning the seat to the Republicans.

District 47

This seat was another Republican leaning district that had been converted to the Democrat side after a close race in 2012. The winner in that race was Linda Stewart, a former Orange County commissioner who defeated her Republican opponent by 4% of the vote. In 2014, the district, all of which is in Orange County, was virtually even in voter registration with the Republicans holding a 109 person margin.

As a member of the House, Stewart had been a progressive legislator who stood up for public schools, protection of the environment, and the rights of women, LGBTQ citizens, and the disabled.

After a contested primary, the Republicans chose as their candidate Mike Miller, a former baseball player for the University of Florida who had been active in several statewide Republican campaigns and who was a marketing director for Rollins College in Winter Park, Florida.

The campaign initially focused on the policy differences between the two candidates and by October 14th, Miller led Stewart by fifteen points, 56% to 41% (Schorsch 2014a).

As the campaign came to an end it became "one of the most negative, if not the most negative State House race in Central Florida" (Terris 2014).

The Stewart campaign challenged Miller's employment status, implying he lied about his position at Rollins College and Miller's team filed an ethics complaint against Stewart, alleging that she failed to report rental income on a property she owned (Kunerth 2014).

From the outset, the Stewart campaign was plagued by missteps in strategy and in implementation. Initially, it decided to use a direct mail-only communications strategy. When the first tracking poll came in, a decision was made to add television. This decision was implemented in the week before absentee ballots hit and the first week of vote-by-mail ballots arrived in voter's hands. In this district, 35% of voters voted by mail and a large portion of those voter saw no television ads from Stewart before voting. This disparity in television ad buying led to a 7% loss in absentee voting. At the end of the campaign Stewart said she was outspent on television by a two to one ratio (Stewart internal campaign documents). The Florida Center for Public Integrity claimed that the Republican Party of Florida spent $394,700 on television on Miller's behalf (Florida Center for Public Integrity 2014).

As was the case with the television campaign, the field organization also started late and had few volunteers and it got fully underway only in the last three weeks of the campaign. Ultimately it hit over 20,000 doors and contacted 35,000 voters. (Stewart internal campaign documents) This effort could not, however, make up for the absence of early contact.

Despite her incumbent status, Stewart was overwhelmed in fundraising. Her own campaign raised less than did that of her opponent and the Republican Party of Florida was able to put substantially greater resources into the race than was the Democratic Party. Overall, Miller outpaced Stewart by nearly $350,000, or $772,253 to $427,722 (Stewart internal campaign records). Furthermore, as was the case in all Democratic races in 2014, voter turnout in the district declined substantially, by 25% compared to the 2012 election (Republicans declined by 19% and Democrats by 32%) and Miller won by 4% of the vote, 36,987 to 30,303.

District 49

The 2012 reapportionment plan centered this new district around the University of Central Florida (UCF) campus in Orlando and the open seat drew two former UCF students to a race where registered Democrats outnumbered Republicans by about 10,000 persons.

Democrat Joe Saunders, who held senior positions at Equality Means Business, the nation's first state-wide corporate equality coalition, defeated Marco Peña, the only two-time Puerto Rican president of the UCF student body, by 12% of the vote. With his election, Saunders, along with fellow

State Representative David Richardson, became the first openly gay member of the Florida State legislature.

As a freshman legislator, Saunders emerged as a leading advocate for public education and as a critic of policies that moved money from public schools into private organizations of charter schools and vouchers. While in the legislature, he supported a bill outlawing huge severance packages for charter school executives. He cosponsored a bill to increase arts education and a second that created health and safety standards in preschools. Saunders' activities earned him the Freshman Lawmaker of the Year award from the Florida Education Association and a leadership award from the Florida Association of Early Learning Coalitions.

As their candidate, the Republicans also nominated an education-oriented candidate and a graduate of UCF, high school track coach Rene "Coach P" Plasencia. Plasencia opposed teacher testing, teacher merit pay, school testing, and standardized end-of-year testing for students. Nevertheless, he sided with Republican Governor Rick Scott in opposing an increase of the minimum wage to $10 per hour and was conservative on many issues, including gun rights, economics, taxes, and job growth (Powers 2014).

Both campaigns ran hard, but Saunders was successful in raising about $100,000 more in campaign funds than did Plasencia. In coordination with the Orange County DEC, the Saunders' field organization also canvassed 76,440 doors and made 33,637 contacts at the door. Some thought that those made by the DEC may have been less effective than those made by the campaign (Green and Gerber 2015). On the phone, the Saunders campaign attempted 26,219 calls and made 2,583 contacts (Saunders internal campaign records).

Like his counterparts in districts 30 and 47, Saunders could not overcome the drop-off in voter turnout that plagued all Democrats in this off year election. While Democrats enjoy a 12% voter registration advantage in the district, they had only a 3% advantage in turnout. In 2012, 59,445 voters cast their ballots in this district. In 2014, those totals dropped to 37,524, the Democratic vote fell by 45% and Plasencia won in an upset by 714 votes.

District 65

Like district 29, this district is solidly Republican and that party's supporters outnumber Democrats by about 25%, or 48,001 to 35,620. It includes the communities of Tarpon Springs, Dunedin, Palm Harbor, and East Lake. Despite its Republican leanings, in 2012 the district had fallen to a Democrat, Carl Zimmerman.

As was also the case in district 29, the Democratic challenger won his 2012 victory under extraordinary circumstances when "racy photos of [his incumbent opponent Peter] Nehr surfaced on the Internet" (Henderson 2013). Zimmerman, a high school journalism teacher, had run against Nehr in two previous elections and lost narrowly, and the partisan characteristics of the district made it unlikely that he would have succeeded in the absence of an event exposing the incumbent to unusual and negative scrutiny.

Thus in 2014, when the base partisanship distribution was undisturbed by extraordinary events, and the candidate of the predominant party conducted a *normal* campaign, Zimmerman was "exposed" (Abramowitz 2011) and fell to first time candidate Chris Sprowls.

Sprowls was an extremely conservative former Assistant State Attorney who ran on opposition to Medicaid expansion, support for charter schools, and pro-life positions on several social issues. He once claimed that "you might be physically better off not to have insurance than Medicaid" (Perry 2014).

While the Zimmerman campaign fought on all levels (television, mail, and on the ground), they were outgunned and overmatched in all these elements. Sprowls outspent Zimmerman on television by $192,323 to $183,607, he "likely sent 3 to 4 times as many mail pieces" as did Zimmerman, and the Zimmerman campaign admitted that "a more robust field program could have benefitted the campaign during the persuasion phase" (Zimmerman internal campaign documents). Finally, Sprowls raised 38% more money than did Zimmerman, $754,320 to $471,129 (Zimmerman internal campaign documents).

In the end, these weaknesses may not have mattered given the partisan make up of the district. In the three previous elections, the Democrats at the top of the ticket lost the two way vote by between 3% and 8.6%, and in 2014 Sprowls won by 4.8% of the vote.

District 112

This district lies at the heart of Miami-Dade County and is a very competitive district with 27,371 Republican registered voters, 29,939 Democrats, and 28,016 unaffiliated. It includes conservative leaning Little Havana and the Rhodes neighborhood, liberal leaning Coconut Grove and Brickell, and mixed communities such as Coral Gables and Key Biscayne. Both parties have targeted the district and have made it a central focus of their efforts to appeal to the increasing Hispanic population in Florida.

In the wake of the 2012 reapportionment, the district was an *open* seat for which Alex Diaz de la Portilla filed as the Republican candidate, and political unknown José Javier Rodríguez filed as a Democrat. Dias de la Portilla was one three brothers who had served in the Florida legislature and had just completed two terms in the Florida Senate where he was the majority leader. While he raised $937,000 dollars for his campaign, his opposition to open carry gun laws and his reputation as a lobbyist was said to contribute to his defeat.

The winner in that race, Jose Javier Rodríguez, was a Harvard trained attorney who had campaigned on supporting public education, encouraging economic growth, and the fresh perspective he would bring to the legislature. He subsequently gained a reputation as skilled debater who was seen as a rising star in Florida political circles. He supported Medicaid expansion and opposed tax breaks for professional sports franchises. He also battled Florida Power and Light over their plan to put up power lines along US Route 1.

In 2014, the Republicans nominated their own version of a rising star to run against Rodríguez. They selected Daniel Diaz Leyva, a real estate attorney and lobbyist who sat on the boards of CHARLEE Homes for Children in Miami-Dade and Banyan Health Systems. His platform included lowering taxes, creating a more favorable environment for businesses, and providing additional vocational and technical training for Floridians.

Both candidates in the 2104 race ran aggressively, with personal on-the-ground efforts and substantial television campaigns, and both political parties supported their respective candidate at high levels. Between July 1st and November 4th, the Rodríguez campaign knocked on 51,206 doors and spoke with 11,030 voters, and made 25,379 phone calls and talked to 2,851 voters (Rodriguez internal campaign records). While the Leyva campaign outspent Rodríguez on television by $291,708 to $270,000 (Rodríguez internal campaign records), the relative parity in spending meant there was little-to-no net advantage to the Republicans.

With an estimated contribution of $439,738 from the Republican Party, Leyva raised $858,995. Rodriguez was also a fundraising machine who generated $338,093 and was supported with $382,175 from the Democratic Party for a total of $718,268. While the $140,000 difference in campaign spending likely made the racer closer than it should have been, it was not enough to change the outcome against an effective candidate with a well-run campaign.

As was the case in districts 29, 30, and 49, President Obama's absence on the presidential ticket contributed to a substantial decline in voter turnout, but in this district, the Democrat was able to overcome this malady and secure a narrow victory, winning by 642 votes out of 33,390 cast. In 2012, 52,248 ballots had been cast.

PATTERNS IN THE OUTCOMES OF
THE FLORIDA LEGISLATIVE RACES

In order to gain perspective on the 2014 legislative races in Florida, we now aggregate the results of the previous analyses into a frame used by other scholars and compare the 2014 to other electoral years in the State. We examine the gains/losses by the party of the president, the success/failure of incumbents in winning re-election, and the level of party success in state legislative elections.

Gains/Loses by the Party of the President

"Downballot" races, both congressional and state legislative, are substantially influenced by the presence or absence of a presidential candidate on the ticket and the party in the White House regularly loses seats in state legislatures in midterm elections (Bibby 1983a and 1983b; Campbell 1986; Little 1998).

While in general Florida conformed to this pattern in 2014, it was in the state House of Representatives and not in the state Senate where the effects were evident.

Barack Obama's Democrats maintained their standing in the state Senate when each of the Party's four incumbents were re-elected. Two of the four, Geraldine Thompson and Oscar Braynon, were challenged in a primary but overcame the challenge and went on to win in the general election. The other two, Darren Soto and Maria Sachs, moved directly into the general election and won those races.

The outcome in the state House of Representatives was very different and the Democrats gave up some of the gains they had made in 2012. They lost the following six seats: House district 29, Mike Clelland; House district 30, Karen Castor Dentel; House district 39, Joe Saunders; House district 47, Linda Stewart; House district 63, Mark Danish; and House district 65, Carl Zimmerman.

In total, the party of the president lost 6 seats in the Florida State Legislature in 2014. This loss conforms to both the national and the Florida *standard* of losses by the party of the president in off year elections.

Incumbency Success

Many observers of American politics express concern about the rate at which incumbents win re-election to their positions. These critics suggest that incumbents use the advantages of their offices to insulate themselves from losing elections and, by doing so, have little incentive to be responsive to the policy concerns of their constituents.

It is certainly the case that incumbency is a primary factor influencing election outcomes, and incumbency success in the 2014 state legislative elections around the nation was high. An analysis by FollowTheMoney showed that throughout the country as a whole "incumbents enjoyed a 91 percent chance of success" (Casey 2016).

In Florida incumbency success in state legislative races was slightly higher. Twenty incumbents ran for re-election in the state Senate and all were re-elected, a 100% success rate. In the House, 104 incumbents sought re-election and seven were defeated, a 93% success. The overall incumbency success rate in Florida was 94.3%, somewhat lower than the 95.6% rate observed in the state in 2012. When 94.3% success is *low* something smells in the electoral system.

Party Success

In 2014, for the tenth consecutive electoral cycle, control of the Florida State Legislature, both the House of Representatives and the Senate, remained under the control of the Republican Party of Florida. The state Senate numbers remained the same as 2012 (26 Republicans and 14 Democrats), while in the Florida House of Representatives, the Republicans increased their majority numbers from 74-46 to 82-37.

Chapter Eight

The 2014 Elections and
the Future of Florida Politics

Competition for seats in American state legislatures in 2014 was "among the lowest ... in the last 40 years" (Klarner 2015). The percentage of people living where a state legislative election was won by 5% or less was the second lowest for state senators since 1972 and the third lowest over that period for state Representatives. The numbers involved were 6.0% for state Senators and 6.5% for state legislatures.

In Florida the comparable numbers were even less encouraging. Only 5% of state Senate races were decided by less than 5% of the vote and even fewer state House races (4.1%) were decided by this margin. Further, 51.7% of the candidates who ran for the state House faced no competition in the general election as did 60% of those who ran for the state Senate. The incumbency success rate in the state Senate was 100% and in the House it was 93.9%. Perhaps most disturbing of all, *the names of more than one third (1/3rd) of all of the people who were elected to the Florida legislature in 2014 did not appear on the ballot at all. They were elected when they paid the filing fee for the office.*

Conditions such as these pose a serious issue for government in the future. In the following paragraphs we identify the extent of this malady and discuss some implications.

LEGISLATIVE COMPETITION IN FLORIDA
AND THE NATION, 1968–2014

The notion of competition as a necessary condition of democracy is widely acknowledged. It is through political competition that citizens are able to express policy choices and hold elected officials accountable for their actions.

In his 1861 *Considerations of Representative Government*, John Stuart Mill (1806-1873) reminds us that "in every government there is some power stronger than all the rest" and in the absence of competition, "the power which is strongest tends to perpetually become the sole power" (Mill 1861, 143; quoted in McDonald and Samples 2006, 1).

The existence of two long periods in Florida politics under these non-competitive conditions—one in which the Democrats were dominant and another in which the Republicans took control—lend validity to these concerns. From the days of Reconstruction in Florida until 1996, the Democrats ruled with very little opposition from Republicans. Beginning with the administration of Jeb Bush in 1998, the Republicans took control of state government and have also governed with little *push back* from Democrats.

Low levels of electoral competition in Florida are endemic, are likely to continue into the foreseeable future, and have, as a result, created unhealthy political conditions in the state.

COMPETITIVENESS IN THE 2014 STATE LEGISLATIVE ELECTIONS: FIVE PERCENT MARGINALITY

Although there is no official definition of a close or competitive election, most political observers use vote margins as one standard and employ 5% or 10% differences as cut-off points. Here we use the 5% standard and present data in table 8.1, showing the extent, or in this case, the limits, of electoral competition in Florida.

In the state legislative races in Florida in 2014, only six races (or 4.2% of the total) were settled by a margin of less than 5%; one of the races was in the state Senate and the other five were in the House of Representatives. The comparable percentages then are 4.2% in the House and 5% in Senate. Put another way, in over 95% of the legislative electorate in Florida in 2014, *there was little or no competition for the seats*.

The low level of competition in Florida has persisted over time. Between 1968 and 2014, there was never an election cycle in which more than 15% of the state House districts were competitive at a level greater than 5%. In the Senate this condition has occurred in only two years. In sum, in 96% of the state legislative elections held in Florida between 1968 and 2014, more than 85% of the electorate has been offered no meaningful choice in their elected official.

Competition in Florida is lower than it is in the nation as a whole and the national totals are nothing to brag about. Table 8.1 shows that in 2014 the percentages of 5% marginality House districts in Florida was 2.3% lower than in the nation as a whole (4.2% to 6.5%), and that the percentages in the Senate was 1% lower than in the nation at large (5% to 6%).

Table 8.1. Electoral Competitiveness in the Florida Legislature (1968–2014)

	Percent 5% Marginality				Percent Incumbent Wins				Percent Uncontested			
	FL House	Nation	FL Senate	Nation	FL House	Nation	FL Senate	Nation	FL House	Nation	FL Senate	Nation
1968	3.4%	9.3%	6.3%	9.5%	94.5%	—	93.8%	—	44.9%	—	14.6%	—
1970	9.2%	10.4%	11.1%	11.1%	96.5%	—	NA	—	55.9%	—	44.4%	—
1972	10.0%	11.0%	5.0%	10.4%	97.2%	92.2%	91.7%	92.4%	34.2%	21.7%	35.0%	21.1%
1974	8.3%	10.2%	9.1%	10.5%	92.7%	88.7%	78.6%	97.2%	52.1%	24.1%	50.0%	27.6%
1976	6.7%	8.3%	15.0%	10.7%	97.8%	92.7%	93.3%	89.7%	53.3%	25.7%	60.0%	29.4%
1978	11.7%	8.6%	0%	8.2%	95.0%	93.3%	100%	92.9%	45.8%	25.4%	34.8%	31.0%
1980	6.7%	8.1%	9.5%	10.9%	96.1%	92.3%	92.3%	90.2%	63.3%	23.9%	38.1%	31.6%
1982	5.8%	8.0%	12.5%	9.1%	94.9%	93.0%	89.3%	93.0%	37.5%	27.6%	47.5%	28.9%
1984	6.7%	7.4%	5.0%	9.4%	94.5%	93.9%	100%	92.0%	54.2%	30.5%	60.0%	33.1%
1986	5.0%	6.8%	27.3%	6.8%	98.9%	96.7%	85.7%	96.6%	45.0%	29.2%	36.4%	33.2%
1988	5.8%	7.0%	4.5%	7.6%	97.0%	96.7%	100%	96.8%	56.7%	31.9%	63.6%	34.1%
1990	6.7%	7.9%	28.6%	9.0%	94.2%	93.6%	92.3%	92.5%	49.2%	25.5%	28.6%	33.2%
1992	14.2%	9.1%	5.0%	9.4%	93.4%	93.7%	81.8%	92.9%	42.5%	27.4%	37.5%	28.4%
1994	10.0%	7.8%	9.1%	8.7%	93.8%	92.4%	88.9%	91.9%	53.3%	26.8%	36.4%	33.1%
1996	7.5%	7.4%	9.5%	7.8%	98.1%	96.2%	100%	95.7%	50.8%	27.3%	47.6%	30.1%
1998	6.7%	6.1%	10.0%	5.6%	96.7%	96.6%	100%	95.8%	62.5%	32.4%	65.0%	37.4%
2000	10.0%	6.6%	10.0%	6.9%	98.1%	97.0%	100%	95.8%	41.7%	32.2%	50.0%	36.0%
2002	2.5%	7.2%	2.5%	7.9%	97.8%	95.3%	95.5%	94.4%	43.3%	36.3%	65.0%	35.0%
2004	3.3%	7.7%	0%	7.4%	100%	96.8%	100%	96.6%	65.0%	35.7%	63.6%	37.0%
2006	6.7%	8.5%	10.0%	8.3%	97.6%	96.6%	100%	96.4%	57.5%	29.0%	65.0%	36.2%
2008	9.2%	7.5%	4.8%	7.2%	100%	97.4%	100%	97.1%	50.8%	34.6%	42.9%	37.0%
2010	2.5%	8.1%	0%	9.0%	93.8%	91.2%	100%	90.9%	40.8%	23.8%	47.8%	33.0%
2012	9.2%	8.1%	0%	2.6%	94.9%	96.1%	95.8%	96.7%	50.0%	36.1%	32.5%	36.4%
2014	4.2%	6.5%	5.0%	6.0%	93.9%	96.5%	100%	97.2%	57.7%	32.8%	60.0%	40.4%

Source: Carl Klarner, 2015, "Competitiveness in State Legislative Elections: 1972-2014, Democracy in Decline: The Collapse of the 'Close Race' in State Legislatures," Ballotpedia, May 6, http:/ballotpedia.org/Competitiveness_in_state_legislative_elections:_1972-2014.

This discrepancy has existed over time. In the House there have been only eight years in which Florida had a higher percentage of 5% marginality districts than did the nation as a whole. And in the Senate there have been only nine such years (table 8.1).

COMPETITIVENESS IN THE 2014 STATE LEGISLATIVE ELECTIONS: INCUMBENCY SUCCESS

Competition for legislative seats in Florida, as throughout the nation, is inhibited by the incumbency factor. Many, if not most legislative seats are held by individuals who won their positions in earlier years and who had substantial advantages when running for re-election. The advantages are such that few opponents risk a try at unsetting them and those who do try are at substantial disadvantages. When large percentages of incumbents hold office, competitiveness decreases. Incumbents usually win re-election and their success rate is a measure of competitiveness; the higher the rate of incumbency success, the lower the competitiveness.

As shown in table 8.1, incumbency success in Florida is very high (and competition is low). In 2014, 93.9% of the incumbents who ran for re-election in the House of Representatives were successful and 100% of incumbent Senators were victorious.

This level of success has persisted over time and stands out against the equally high rates in other state legislatures around the nation. In every year between 1968 and 2014, the percentages of incumbents who successfully sought re-election to the Florida House of Representatives exceeded 90%. And in the state Senate these percentages were exceeded in all but five of the twenty-four years involved. In only three of the twenty-four years were greater percentages of members of state's lower chambers around the nation re-elected in higher percentages than in Florida and in only five years was this the case regarding state Senates. In effect, if you get elected to the Florida state legislature, you stay in office until term limits require you to retire or until you voluntarily give up your seat.

COMPETITIVENESS IN THE 2014 STATE LEGISLATIVE ELECTIONS: UNCONTESTED SEATS

To restate an earlier observation, the *names of more than one third (34.2%) of the candidates who were elected to the Florida legislature in 2014 did not appear on the ballot in that year.*

These candidates ran unopposed throughout the entire electoral cycle; the primary and the general elections. In eight of twenty Senate races and in 40 of 120 House races, candidates were elected simply by signing a form and paying a filing fee. No citizen had an opportunity to express an opinion about the candidate's qualifications for the office.

The Florida numbers are comparable to similar figures for legislatures throughout the United States, which was 36% (Stepleton 2016).

The opposition that over one half of all successful candidates for Florida legislative seats did face came only in their own party's primary. The winners, 57.7% in the House of Representatives and 60.0% of those in the state Senate, ran without opposition in the general election.

The numbers of unopposed races for the general election in Florida are substantially higher than for comparable races around the nation. In 2014, general election races for state House seats around the nation saw only 32.8% unopposed while in state Senates, the number was 40% unopposed.

The percentages of unopposed races for the Florida state legislature have been much higher than those from other states for over twenty years. As the data in table 8.1 show, the percentages of unopposed candidates in Florida are usually in the 50% range in the House while the percentages nationwide fall in the 20% to 30% range. In the Senate, the differences are similar.

MONETARY FACTORS IN ELECTORAL COMPETITION

Much of the disparity in the outcomes of state legislative races stems from the uneven distribution of monetary resources among candidates. Other things equal, the candidate with the most money has an advantage over the candidate who has less money. In particular, a money advantage allows a candidate to communicate more often and more effectively with voters, a crucial factor in state legislative races which are low visibility, low information contests.

In Florida, Democrats are particularly disadvantaged in comparison to Republicans, who typically raise substantially more money for their campaigns than do Democrats. Furthermore, and especially important, the advantage applied to virtually every candidate. As shown in table 8.2, in 95% of the state House races, the top candidates raised more than twice the money as the next candidate. In the state Senate the disparity was only slightly less, at 92%.

Table 8.2 also shows that substantially larger numbers of both individuals and organizations contribute to top candidates than to the next highest ranked candidate, thus decreasing the likelihood of a competitive election. In the

Table 8.2. Monetary Competitiveness in Florida (2000–2014)

	State House			State Senate		
Year	Monetary	Individual Support	Non-Individual Support	Monetary	Individual Support	Non-Individual Support
2014	92%	82%	95%	95%	100%	100%
2012	95%	78%	97%	85%	85%	97%
2010	89%	73%	96%	87%	96%	96%
2008	92%	76%	95%	95%	85%	85%
2006	92%	89%	94%	95%	85%	85%
2004	96%	92%	97%	100%	95%	100%
2002	91%	82%	97%	87%	85%	91%
2000	82%	79%	95%	76%	86%	90%

Monetary: Percent of seats where top candidate raised more than twice the money as the next candidate; *Individual Support*: Percent of seats where the top candidate has more than twice the number of contributors as the next highest candidate; and *Non-Individual Support*: Percent of seats where the top candidate has more than twice the number of non-individual contributors as the next highest candidate. *Sources*, Linda Casey. 2016, "2013 and 2014: Money and Incumbency in State Legislative Races," *FollowThe-Money*, March 9, https://www.followthemoney.org/research/institute-reports/2013-and-2014-money-and-incumbency-in-state-legislative-races/.

Senate, top candidates had more than twice the number of both individual and non-individual contributors in *all* (100%) of the races. In the House, this was the case for individual supporters in 82% of the contests and for organizational contributors in 95% of the races.

In the face of disparities such as these, the level of competitiveness in Florida's legislative elections is unlikely to improve and as indicated by Mill (1861), "the power which is strongest" is likely to "become the sole power."

References

Abdill, Rick. 2012. "Mitt Romney Asks Rick Scott to Stop Bragging About How Great Things Are Going." *Broward/Palm Beach New Times*. June 21. http://www. browardpalmbeach.com/news/mitt-romney-asks-rick-scott-to-stop-bragging-about-how-great-things-are-going-6473329 (accessed July 31, 2017).

Abramowitz, Alan. 2011. "Right Turn: The 2010 Midterm Elections." In *Pendulum Swing*, edited by Larry J. Sabato, 49-50. Boston: Longman.

American Presidency Project. 2017. http://www.presidency.ucsb.edu/ (accessed July 31, 2017).

Associated Press (AP). 2014a. "Exit Poll and Related Survey Methodology—2014 General Election." http://surveys.ap.org/exitpolls/ (accessed July 31, 2017).

———. 2014b. "Charlie Crist's Campaign Focuses on South Florida." October 22. http://wusfnews.wusf.usf.edu/post/charlie-crists-campaign-focuses-on-south-florida (accessed August 4, 2017).

———. 2014c. "Medical Marijuana Initiative Defeated in Florida." *Florida Today*. Nov 4. http://www.floridatoday.com/story/news/politics/elections/2014/11/04/medical-marijuana-initiative-defeated-in-florida/18500723/ (accessed July 31, 2017).

Auslen, Michael. 2016. "Old Questions Resurface as Attorney General Pam Bondi Endorses Trump." *Miami Herald*. March 14. http://www.miamiherald.com/news/politics-government/election/article65995972.html (accessed August 19, 2017).

Ball, Molly. 2014. "Is This What Post-Partisanship Looks Like?" *Atlantic*, March 11. https://www.theatlantic.com/politics/archive/2014/03/is-this-what-post-partisanship-looks-like/284350/ (accessed August 4, 2017).

Ballotpedia. 2014. "Florida Right to Medical Marijuana Imitative, Amendment 2. (2014)." *Ballotpedia*. https://ballotpedia.org/Florida_Right_to_Medical_Marijuana_Initiative,_Amendment_2_(2014) (accessed July 31, 2017).

Barone, Michael, and Richard E. Cohen. 2004. *Almanac of American Politics: The Senators, the Representatives, and the Governors; Their Records and Election Results, Their States and Districts*. Washington, DC: National Journal Group.

Bender, Michael C. 2012. Interview with Mike Slade. "The GOP's Rick Scott Problem." July 26. https://www.bloomberg.com/news/articles/2012-07-26/the-gops-rick-scott-problem (accessed August 4, 2017).

Berman, Russell. 2015. "Florida Struggles to Pay the Tab for Rejecting Obamacare." *Atlantic*. May 8. https://www.theatlantic.com/politics/archive/2015/05/florida-struggles-to-pay-the-tab-for-rejecting-obamacare/392678/ (accessed July 31, 2017).

Bibby, John F. 1983a. "Patterns in Midterm Gubernatorial and State Legislative Elections." *Public Opinion* 6 (February-March):41-46.

———. 1983b. "State House Elections in Midterm." In *The American National Elections of 1982*, edited by Thomas E. Mann and Norman J. Ornstein, 111-32. Washington, DC: American Enterprise Institute.

Bloggytown. 2014. "Equality Florida PAC Endorses Not-Gay Charlie Crist for Governor (UPDATE: So Does HRC)." *Orlando Weekly* (blog). June 12. https://www.orlandoweekly.com/Blogs/archives/2014/06/12/equality-florida-pac-endorses-not-gay-charlie-crist-for-governor-update-so-does-hrc (accessed August 2, 2017).

Bousquet, Steve. 2014a. "Gov. Scott Draws Two Republican Challengers in Re-Election Bid." *Tampa Bay Times*. June 16. http://www.tampabay.com/news/politics/gubernatorial/gov-scott-draws-two-republican-challengers-in-reelection-bid/2184576 (accessed July 24, 2017).

Bousquet, Steve. 2014b. "Charlie Crist Stakes Election Victory on Broward County Turnout." *Tampa Bay Times*. October 14. http://www.tampabay.com/news/politics/legislature/charlie-crist-stakes-election-victory-on-broward-county-turnout/2202092 (accessed August 1, 2017).

Bousquet, Steve, and Michael Auslen. 2016. "Pam Bondi's Career Path Could Lead to Trump's White House." *Bradenton Herald*. December 2. http://www.bradenton.com/news/politics-government/article118433923.html (accessed August 1, 2017).

Bousquet, Steve, and Marc Caputo. 2014. "Charlie Crist vs. Nan Rich, A Democratic Primary Devoid of a Campaign." *Tampa Bay Times*. August 24. http://www.tampabay.com/news/politics/stateroundup/charlie-crist-vs-nan-rich-the-democratic-primary-campaign-devoid-of-a/2194367 (accessed August 4, 2017).

Bukley, Ron. 2014. "Murphy, Domino Face Off for Congressional Seat." *Town-Crier*. September 19. http://gotowncrier.com/2014/09/murphy-domino-face-off-for-congress-in-district-18/ (accessed August 1, 2017).

Campbell, James E. 1986. "Presidential Coattails and Midterm Losses in State Legislative Elections." *American Political Science Review* 80(1): 45-63.

Campus Election Engagement Project. 2014. "Rick Scott vs. Charlie Crist: Nonpartisan Candidate Guide for Florida Governor's Race 2014." (blog). October 19. http://www.huffingtonpost.com/campus-election-engagement-project/rick-scott-vs-charlie-cri_b_5974442.html (accessed August 6, 2017).

Caputo, Marc. 2013. "Tea Party Rep. Trey Radel Busted For Cocaine in D.C." *Miami Herald*. November 19. http://www.miamiherald.com/news/state/article1957627.html (accessed August 1, 2017).

Caputo, Marc. 2014. "The 2014 Governor's Race Votes and Ad Spending by Florida Media Market." *Miami Herald*. November 25. http://miamiherald.typepad.

com/nakedpolitics/2014/11/the-2014-governors-race-votes-and-ad-spending-by-florida-media-market-.html (accessed August 1, 2017).

Casey, Linda. 2016. "2013 and 2014: Money and Incumbency in State Legislative Races." *FollowTheMoney.* March 9. https://www.followthemoney.org/research/institute-reports/2013-and-2014-money-and-incumbency-in-state-legislative-races/ (accessed August 1, 2017).

Clozel, Lalita, 2014. "Cash for Challengers: Some Turn the Tables, Outraising Incumbents." *OpenSecrets.org.* November 1. https://www.opensecrets.org/news/2014/11/cash-for-challengers-some-turn-the-tables-outraising-incumbents/ (accessed August 1, 2017).

The Cook Political Report. 2107. *CookPolitical.com.* http://cookpolitical.com/ (accessed August 21, 2017).

Cordiero, Monivette. 2016. "Medical Marijuana Will Be Back On the Ballot This Fall and It Seems the Opposition Has Gone Up In Smoke." *Orlando Weekly.* April 20. https://www.orlandoweekly.com/orlando/medical-marijuana-will-be-back-on-the-ballot-this-fall-and-it-seems-the-opposition-has-gone-up-in-smoke/Content?oid=2485404&showFullText=true (accessed August 1, 2017).

CNN. 2014. "America's Choice 2014: Election Center." *CNN.com.* November 6. http://www.cnn.com/election/2014/results/state/FL/governor/# (accessed August 21, 2017).

Crew, Robert E., Jr. 2013. *The 2010 Elections in Florida: It's the Economy, Stupid!.* Lanham, MD: University Press of America.

Crew, Robert E., Jr., and Mary Ruggiero Anderson. 2016. *The 2012 Elections in Florida: Obama Wins and Democrats Make Strides in Downticket Races.* Lanham, MD: University Press of America.

Crew. Robert E., Jr., Alexandra Cockerham, and Edward James, III. 2017. "A Blue Dot in a Field of Red: Gwen Graham Wins Florida's Second Congressional District." In *Races, Reforms and Policy: Implications of the 2014 Midterm Elections*, edited by Christopher J. Galdieri, Tauna S. Sisco, and Jennifer C. Lucas. Akron, OH. University of Akron Press.

Cubit. 2016. "Florida Demographics." Derived from the U.S. Census Bureau and Florida Department of State, Elections Division, "Annual Estimates of the Resident Population: April 1, 2010 to July 1, 2016." http://factfinder2.census.gov. Available online at https://www.florida-demographics.com/counties_by_population (accessed August 4, 2017).

Derby, Kevin. 2014a. "Carl Domino Questions Patrick Murphy's Independence." *Sunshine State News.* October 6. http://www.sunshinestatenews.com/story/carl-domino-questions-patrick-murphys-independence (accessed August 2, 2017).

Derby, Kevin. 2014b. "Carlos Curbelo Edges Joe Garcia, Flips Congressional Seat to the GOP." *Sunshine State News.* November 3. http://www.sunshinestatenews.com/story/carlos-curbelo-edges-joe-garcia-flips-congressional-seat-gop (accessed August 2, 2017).

Deslatte, Aaron. 2004. "Rick Scott Launches $2.2M Ad Buy to Talk About Families." *Orlando Sentinel.* March 11. http://www.orlandosentinel.com/news/politics/political-pulse/os-rick-scott-launches-22-mil-ad-buy-to-talk-about-families-20140311-post.html (accessed August 2, 2017).

DownWithTyranny. 2014. "Dennis Ross Taunts His Moderate Tampa Bay Constituents That He's 'More Conservative Than Alan West.'" *DownWithTyranny!* (blog). June 21. http://downwithtyranny.blogspot.com/2014/06/dennis-ross-taunts-his-moderate-tampa.html?m=0 (accessed August 2, 2017).

Dunkelberger, Lloyd. 2014. "Crist-Scott Race is Nation's Costliest." *Herald Tribune.* October 3. http://politics.heraldtribune.com/2014/10/03/crist-scott-race-nations-costliest/ (accessed August 2, 2017).

FairVote. 2014. "Dubious Democracy 1994." *FairVote.org.* http://www.fairvote.org/dubious_democracy (accessed August 21, 2017).

Farrington, Brendan. 2013. "Charlie Crist to Run as Democrat Against Rick Scott for FL Governor." *Christian Science Monitor.* November 2. https://www.csmonitor.com/USA/Latest-News-Wires/2013/1102/Charlie-Crist-to-run-as-Democrat-against-Rick-Scott-for-FL-governor (accessed August 2, 2017).

Florida Center for Public Integrity. 2014. "Who's Calling the Shots? State Ad Wars Tracker: TV Ads in 2014 State Races." December 8. https://www.publicintegrity.org/2014/09/21/15574/florida (accessed August 2, 2017).

Florida Department of Agriculture and Consumer Services. 2017. "About." *Freshfromflorida.com.* http://www.freshfromflorida.com/About/ (accessed August 7, 2017).

Florida Department of State. 2014a. "2014 General Election, Election Number: 10218." http://dos.myflorida.com/media/696917/early-voting-and-vote-by-mail-report-2014-gen.pdf (accessed August 4, 2017).

———. 2014b. *Division of Elections.* "Voter Turnout by County." https://enight.elections.myflorida.com (accessed August 4, 2017).

———. 2017a. *Division of Elections.* "Election Reporting System." https://results.elections.myflorida.com/ (accessed August 4, 2017).

———. 2017b. *Division of Elections.* "Voter Turnout by Population." http://dos.myflorida.com/elections/ (accessed August 4, 2017).

———. 2017c. *Division of Elections.* "Voter Turnout." http://dos.myflorida.com/elections/data-statistics/elections-data/voter-turnout/ (accessed August 21, 2017).

Florida House of Representatives. 2011. *An Act Related to Elections.* CS/CS/HB 1355. Chapter No. 2011-40. May 19. https://www.flsenate.gov/Session/Bill/2011/1355 (accessed August 4, 2017).

FollowTheMoney.org. 2014. https://www.followthemoney.org/ (accessed August 21, 2017).

Fox, Lauren. 2014. "Florida's Special Election Remains a Test for Republicans and Democrats." *U.S. News.* June 27. https://www.usnews.com/news/blogs/ballot-2014/2014/03/11/floridas-special-election-remains-a-test-for-republicans-and-democrats (accessed August 2, 2017).

Franz, Michael M., and Travis N. Ridout. 2010. "Political Advertising and Persuasion in the 2004 and 2008 Presidential Elections." *American Politics Research* 38(2): 303-29.

Gallup. N.d. "Obama Job Approval (Weekly)." *Gallup.* http://www.gallup.com/poll/125729/obama-job-approval-weekly.aspx (accessed August 2, 2017).

Gibson, William E. 2014a. "Frankel and Spain Clash in Swing District." *Palm Beach Sun Sentinel.* October 2. http://www.sun-sentinel.com/local/palm-beach/boynton-beach/fl-election-frankel-spain-20141001-story.html (accessed August 2, 2017).

———. 2014b. "Frederica Wilson Seeks Re-election Against GOP Opponent." *Sun Sentinel.* October 9. http://www.sun-sentinel.com/news/politics/fl-election-neree-wilson-20141008-story.html (accessed August 2, 2017).

———. 2014c. "Wasserman Schultz, Kaufman, Race a Clear Contrast." October 9. http://www.sun-sentinel.com/news/politics/fl-election-wasserman-schultz-kaufman-20141008-story.html (accessed August 8, 2017).

Gillin, Joshua. 2014. "Medical Marijuana Amendment Was More Popular Than Winning Governors, Group Says." *Politifact Florida.* November 13. http://www.politifact.com/florida/statements/2014/nov/13/united-care/medical-marijuana-amendment-was-more-popular-winni/ (accessed August 2, 2017).

GovTrack. 2017. "Tracking the Congress, Engaging Democracy." *Civic Impulse, LLC.* https://www.govtrack.us/congress/members (accessed August 18, 2017).

Green, Donald P., and Alan S. Gerber. 2008. *Get Out the Vote: How to Increase Voter Turnout.* 3rd rev. ed. Washington, DC: Brookings Institution Press.

Greenberg, Jeffrey Alexander. 2015. "Murphey vs Domino in Florida." *Vanderbilt Undergraduate Research Journal: Humanities and Social Sciences* 10 (Fall): 1-14. http://ejournals.library.vanderbilt.edu/index.php/vurj/article/view/4076 (accessed August 19, 2017).

Haberman, Maggie. 2015. "Michael Bloomberg Targets Pam Bondi, Other Attorneys General With Ads on Carbon Emissions." *Tampa Bay Times.* November 6. http://www.tampabay.com/news/politics/stateroundup/michael-bloomberg-targets-pam-bondi-other-attorneys-general-with-ads-on/2252957 (accessed August 2, 2017).

Henderson, Jeff. 2013. "Hot House Contest in the Making: Dem Incumbent vs. GOP Prosecutor Sprowls." *Sunshine State News.* April 10. http://dev2.sunshinestatenews.com/node/5296493 (accessed August 2, 2017).

———. 2014. "HD 30: Can Bob Cortes Overcome Karen Castor-Dentel's Name Advantages?" *Sunshine State News,* October 14. http://dev2.sunshinestatenews.com/node/5932984 (accessed August 2, 2017).

Herron, Michael C., and Daniel A. Smith. 2014. "Race, Party, and the Consequences of Restricting Early Votinhttp://www.pbs.org/newshour/updates/florida-race-highlights-shadowy-role-super-pacs/g in Florida in the 2012 General Election." *Political Research Quarterly* 67(3): 646-65.

Holden, Zach. 2014. "2013 and 2014: Monetary Competitiveness in State Legislative Races." *FollowTheMoney.* March 9. https://www.followthemoney.org/research/institute-reports/2013-and-2014-monetary-competitiveness-in-state-legislative-races/ (accessed August 19, 2017).

Hysocki@News-Press.com. 2014. "Rivals Link Clawson to Sex Offender; Victim's Mother Asks Them to Stop." *New-Press.com. USA Today.* April 9. http://www.news-press.com/story/news/politics/2014/04/08/election-2014-rivals-link-clawson-to-sex-offender/7492565/ (accessed August 19, 2017).

Isenstadt, Alex. 2012. "Allen West's Smashmouth Politics." October 15. http://www. politico.com/story/2012/10/wests-blunt-talk-at-crux-of-reelection-fight-082433 (accessed August 8, 2017).

———. 2104. "Jolly Defeats Sink in Florida 13th." *Politico*. March 11. http://www. politico.com/story/2014/03/david-jolly-alex-sink-florida-special-election-2014-104543 (accessed August 2, 2017).

Jaffe, Alexandra. 2014. "Drama Roils Race to Replace Rep. Bill Young." *The Hill*. January 8. http://thehill.com/blogs/ballot-box/senate-races/194716-drama-roils-race-to-replace-rep-bill-young-in-florida (accessed August 19, 2017).

Kam, Dara. 2011. "Early On, Florida Attorney General Pam Bondi Shows Ambition." *Palm Beach Post.* October 8. http://www.palmbeachpost.com/news/state—regional/ early-florida-attorney-general-pam-bondi-shows-ambition/twHhNzyGm3StKb JSo93uXO/ (accessed November 14, 2014).

King, Ledyard. 2014. "Dirty Politics: Republican Primary for House Takes Nasty Turn." *News Press*. March 21. http://www.news-press.com/story/news/politics/2014/03/22/ dirty-politics/6720775/ (accessed August 2, 2017).

Klarner, Carl E. 2015. "Competitiveness in State Legislative Elections: 1972-2014, Democracy in Decline: The Collapse of the 'Close Race' in State Legislatures." *Ballotpedia*. May 6. http://ballotpedia.org/Competitiveness_in_State_Legislative_ Elections:_1972-2014 (accessed August 2, 2017).

Klas, Mary Ellen, 2014. "Florida Supreme Court Approves Congressional Map Drawn by Challengers." *Miami Herald*. October, 2. http://www.miamiherald.com/ news/politics-government/state-politics/article47576450.html (accessed August 19, 2017).

Kroll, Andy. 2011. "Who's the Most Unpopular Governor in America." *Mother Jones*. May 31. http://www.motherjones.com/politics/2011/05/republican-governor-unpopular-obama-president/ (accessed July 24, 2017).

Kunerth, Jeff. 2014. "Miller's Employment Claim, Stewart's Land Become Issues in District 47 Race." *Orlando Sentinel.* October 29. http://www.orlandosentinel. com/news/breaking-news/os-miller-stewart-trade-accusations-20141029-story. html (accessed August 2, 2017).

LaFauci. Trevor. 2014. "Busted: Florida Republicans' 212 Redistricting Plan Thrown Out by Federal Judge." *Politicususa*. July 11. http://www.politicususa. com/2014/07/11/busted-florida-republicans-2012-redistricting-plan-thrown-federal-judge.html (accessed August 2, 2017).

Leary, Alex. 2014. "VA Investigation Gives Low-Key Rep. Jeff Miller the Spotlight." *Tampa Bay Times*. May 21. http://www.tampabay.com/news/politics/national/jeff-miller-low-key-florida-congressman-breaks-through-with-va/2180812 (accessed July 31, 2017).

Little, Thomas H. 1998. "On the Coattails of a Contract: RNC Activities and Republican Gains in the 1994 State Legislative Elections." *Political Research Quarterly* 51(1): 173-90.

Lush, Tamara. 2014. "Republican Atwater Expected to Easily Retain Florida CFO Seat." *Insurance Journal*. October, 28. http://www.insurancejournal.com/news/ southeast/2014/10/28/344867.htm (accessed August 2, 2017).

Man, Anthony. 2014a. "When Charlie Crist Shows Up to Campaign, Republicans Are Sure to Follow." *Sun Sentinel*. September 27. http://www.sun-sentinel.com/news/fl-crist-scott-campaign-shadow-20140927-story.html (accessed August 2, 2017).

———. 2014b. "8 Takeaways from Rick Scott's Win Over Charlie Crist." *Sun Sentinel*. November 5. http://www.sun-sentinel.com/news/fl-florida-governor-lessons-20141105-story.html (accessed August 2, 2017).

Manjarres, Javier. 2014. "Wasserman Schultz is Invincible, Will Win Re-election." *Shark Tank*. October 15. http://shark-tank.com/2014/10/15/wasserman-schultz-invincible-will-win-re-election/ (accessed August 2, 2017).

March, William. 2013. "Rick Scott Claims Responsibility for Economic Recovery, Experts Debunk." *Huffington Post/Tampa Tribune*. September 22. Updated November 22. http://www.huffingtonpost.com/2013/09/22/rick-scott-economic-recovery_n_3970850.html (accessed August 2, 2017).

March, William. 2014. "Cohn Blasts US Rep. Dennis Ross for not Having Office in Hillsborough." *Tbo. Times Publishiing*. August 15. http://www.tbo.com/news/politics/cohn-blasts-us-rep-dennis-ross-for-not-having-office-in-hillsborough-20140815/ (accessed August 19, 2017).

Mazzei, Patrick, and Amy Sherman. 2012. "In South Florida Congressional Races, David Garcia Loses to Joe Garcia, Allen West Appears to Fall to Patrick Murphy." *Miami Herald*. November 7. http://www.miamiherald.com/news/politics-government/article1944340.html (accessed August 19, 2017).

McDonald, Michael P., and John Samples. 2006. The Marketplace of Democracy: Electoral Competition and American Politics. Washington, DC. Brookings Institution Press.

Meacham, Andrew. 2014. "Bill Young's First Family Emerges to Tell Their Story." *Tampa Bay Times*. January 4. http://www.tampabay.com/news/bill-youngs-first-family-emerges-to-tell-their-story/2159685 (accessed August 2, 2017).

Miami Herald. 2013. "Sachs Maintains Broward Residency by renting Condo From Consultant." *Naked Politics*. March 29. http://miamiherald.typepad.com/nakedpolitics/2013/03/sachs-maintains-broward-residency-by-renting-condo-from-consultant.html (accessed August 19, 2017).

Mill, John Stuart. *Considerations on Representative Government*. London: Parker, Son, and Bourn, 1861.

Mitchell, Tia, and Nate Monroe. 2014. "Rick Scott Defeats Charlie Crist in Close Race for Florida Governor." *Florida Times-Union*. November 4. http://jacksonville.com/news/florida/2014-11-04/story/rick-scott-defeats-charlie-crist-close-race-florida-governor (accessed August 2, 2017).

Montanaro, Domenico, Terrence Burlij, Rachel Wellford, and Simone Pathe. 2014. "Florida Race Highlights Shadowy Role of Super PACs. *PBS Newshour*. April 22. http://www.pbs.org/newshour/updates/florida-race-highlights-shadowy-role-super-pacs/ (accessed August 19, 2017).

National Journal. 2017. "Our Mission." *National Journal.* N.d. https://www.nationaljournal.com/ (accessed August 19, 2017).

NBC News. 2014. "Decision 2014: Exit Poll Results." *NBC News*. N.d. http://www.nbcnews.com/politics/elections/2014/FL/governor/exitpoll (accessed August 2, 2017).

Nevins, Buddy. 2014. "With Crist's Loss, Demos Are Dead for Decades." *Broward-Beat.com* (blog). November 5. https://www.browardbeat.com/with-crists-loss-demos-are-dead-for-decade/ (accessed August 2, 2017).

Open Secrets. 2017. "Election Overview." *Open Secrets.org*. http://www.opensecrets.org/overview/reelect.php (accessed August 7, 2017).

Perry, Mitch. 2014. "HD 65 GOP Rep Candidate Chris Sprowls Cites Study That Says It's Better To Have No Insurance Than Medicaid." *Creative Loafing Tampa Bay*. August 27. http://www.cltampa.com/news-views/article/20758627/hd-65-gop-rep-chris-sprowls-says-its-better-to-have-no-insurance-than-medicaid (accessed August 2, 2017).

Pew Research Center. 2014. "Religion and Public Life: Religious Landscape Study, Adults in Florida." *Pew Research Center*. N.d. http://www.pewforum.org/religious-landscape-study/state/florida/ (accessed August 2, 2017).

Pipsorcle. 2013. "Fl-11: Meet David Koller Challenger to Rep. Richard Nugent." *Daily Kos*. November 29. https://www.dailykos.com/stories/2013/11/29/1259078/-FL-11-Meet-David-Koller-Democratic-Challenger-to-Rep-Richard-Nugent-Monday-Dec-2-at-O

Powers, Scott. 2014a. "Democrat Neuman Lying Low in Congressional Race against Mica. *Orlando Sentinel*. September 24. http://www.orlandosentinel.com/news/politics/os-john-mica-wes-neuman-missing-20140924-story.html (accessed August 21, 2017).

Powers, Scott. 2014b. "Race Pits Webster's Experience vs. McKenna's Energy." *Orlando Sentinel*. October 20. http://www.orlandosentinel.com/news/politics/os-election-congress-d10-webster-mckenna-20141008-story.html (accessed August 2, 2017).

Powers, Scott. 2014c. "Grayson, Platt in Sharp Contrast in Congressional Race." *Orlando Sentinel*. October 9. http://www.orlandosentinel.com/news/politics/os-election-congress-grayson-platt-20141006-story.html (accessed August 19, 2017).

Quinnipiac University Poll. 2014. "Crist Has 15-Point Compassion Lead in Florida." April 30. https://poll.qu.edu/florida/release-detail?ReleaseID=2036 (accessed August 4, 2017).

RedState. 2014. *RedState.com*. October. http://www.redstate.com/ (accessed August 21, 2017).

Rumpf, Sarah. 2015. "Florida GOP Chairman, 'This State is Going Red in 2016.'" *Brietbart.com*. May 15. http://www.breitbart.com/big-government/2015/05/15/florida-gop-chairman-this-state-is-going-red-in-2016/ (accessed August 1, 2017).

Schorsch, Peter. 2014a. "Mike Miller Slips 5 Points, Leads Representative Linda Stewart by 10 In New HD 47 Poll." *SaintPetersBlog*. October 29. http://saintpetersblog.com/mike-miller-slips-5-points-leads-rep-linda-stewart-10-new-hd-47-poll/ (accessed August 2, 2017).

———. 2014b. "The Ultimate Post-Mortem: 16 Reasons Why Charlie Crist Fell Short." November 6. *SaintPetersBlog*. http://saintpetersblog.com/10/ (accessed August 2, 2017).

Sharockman, Aaron. 2010. "Alan Grayson Calls Opponent 'Taliban Dan Webster' in Stinging New TV Ad." *Politfacts Florida*. September 25. http://www.politifact.

com/florida/statements/2010/sep/28/alan-grayson/alan-grayson-calls-opponent-taliban-daniel-webster/ (accessed August 19, 2017).

Sides, John, and Lynn Vavreck. 2013. *The Gamble: Choice and Chance in the 2012 Presidential Election.* Princeton, NJ: Princeton University Press.

Siegelbaum, Debbie. 2014. "Florida's Space Race: The Politicians Battling Over the Cosmos." *BBC News Magazine.* October 20. http://www.bbc.com/news/magazine-29654854 (accessed August 2, 2017).

Smith, Adam C. 2013. "Alex Smith is Running for C.W. Bill Young's Congressional Seat, Will Move to Pinellas." *Tampa Bay Times.* October 30. http://www.tampabay.com/news/politics/national/alex-sink-announcement/2149702 (accessed August 22, 2017).

Smith, Adam C., and Marc Caputo. 2014. "How Rick Scott Won Re-Election as Florida Governor." *Tampa Bay Times*, November 5. http://www.tampabay.com/news/politics/stateroundup/how-rick-scott-won-re-election-as-florida-governor/2205342 (accessed August 2, 2017).

Smith, Adam C., Steve Bousquet, and Katie Sanders. 2014. "Florida Gov. Rick Scott defeats Charlie Crist for Re-election." *Tampa Bay Times,* November 4. http://www.tampabay.com/news/politics/stateroundup/gov-rick-scott-leads-charlie-crist-in-early-returns/2205127 (accessed August 2, 2017).

Stepleton, J. T. 2016. "Competitiveness Index How-To." *FollowTheMoney.* September 29. https://www.followthemoney.org/research/blog/competitiveness-index (accessed August 2, 2017).

Sweeney, Dan. 2014a. "Attorney General's Race: Stark Differences Between Bondi, Sheldon." *Sun Sentinel.* October 14. http://www.sun-sentinel.com/news/politics/fl-election-attorney-general-bondi-sheldon-20141014-story.html (accessed August 19, 2017).

Sweeney, Dan. 2014b. "Sachs Defeats Bogdanoff in Tight Race." *Sun Sentinel.* November 4. http://www.sun-sentinel.com/news/politics/fl-election-bogdanoff-sachs-20141104-story.html (accessed August 19, 2017).

Tampa Bay Times. 2014a. "Florida Governor (Republican): Yinka Abosede Adeshina, Elizabeth Cuevas-Neunder, Rick Scott." *Tampa Bay Times.* August 14. http://www.placead.tampabay.com/news/politics/florida-governor-republican-yinka-abosede-adeshina-elizabeth/2192978 (accessed August 4, 2017).

Tampa Bay Times. 2014b. "Know Your Candidates." *Tampa Bay Times.* N.d. http://www.tampabay.com/news/politics/kyc/floridas-us-house-district-17-william-bronson-d-tom-rooney-r/1256912 (accessed August 19, 2017).

Terris, Ben. 2014. "Survival of a Salesman: Charlie Crist Tries to Get Back Where He Once Was." *Washington Post.* February 19. https://www.washingtonpost.com/lifestyle/style/survival-of-a-salesman-charlie-crist-tries-to-get-back-where-he-once-was/2014/02/19/80ccba28-98c0-11e3-80ac-63a8ba7f7942_story.html?utm_term=.7ece8fc0ad64 (accessed August 2, 2017).

Topaz, Jonathan. 2014. "Poll: Obama Hits Lowest Approval." *Politico.* October 15. http://www.politico.com/story/2014/10/poll-obama-approval-rating-111902 (accessed August 2, 2017).

Torres, Frank. 2017. "Castor-Dentel Goes Negative Over Education in House 30 TV Ad." September 23. *Orlando Political Observer*. http://orlando-politics. com/2014/09/23/castor-dentel-goes-negative-over-education-in-house-30-tv-ad/ (accessed August 2, 2017).

Turner, Jim. 2014. Interview with Susan MacManus. "Democrats Lack Attention, Coverage in Primary for AG Job." *Florida Times-Union*. August 15. http://jacksonville. com/news/politics/2014-08-15/story/democrats-lack-attention-coverage-primary-ag-job (accessed August 2, 2017).

U.S. Census Bureau. http://factfinder2.census.gov (accessed August 5, 2017).

U.S. Congress. 2010. *Affordable Care Act*. 111th Cong. 2nd sess. Public Law 111-148. *U.S. Statutes at Large* 124 (March 23): 119-1025.

U.S. Supreme Court. 2015. *Obergefell et al. v. Hodges, Director, Ohio Department of Health et al*. Decided June 26, 2015. No. 14-556, 1-8. https://www.supremecourt. gov/opinions/14pdf/14-556_3204.pdf (accessed August 2, 2017).

Van Sickler, Michael. 2013. "Democrat George Sheldon Challenging Attorney General Pam Bondi." *Tampa Bay Times*. October 21. http://www.tampabay.com/news/ politics/elections/democrat-george-sheldon-challenging-attorney-general-pam-bondi/2148324 (accessed August 19, 2017).

Vogel, Mike. 2013. "Florida's Hispanic Population: Diverse, Powerful and Political, Hispanics in Florida Are Not Easy to Pigeonhole." *Florida Trend*. April 30. http://www.floridatrend.com/article/15528/floridas-hispanic-population?page=1 (accessed August 2, 2017).

Whitaker, Morgan. 2014. "Charlie Crist Reveals the Real Reason He Left Republican Party." *MSNBC*. May 7. http://www.msnbc.com/politicsnation/charlie-crist-racism-why-he-left-gop (accessed August 2, 2017).

Wikipedia. 2017. "United States Congressional Delegations from Florida." https://en.wikipedia.org/wiki/United_States_congressional_delegations_from_ Florida#2003_.E2.80.93_2013:_25_seats (accessed August 7, 2017).

Index

Page references for figures are italicized.

About the Authors

Mary Ruggiero Anderson is chair and associate professor, Department of Political Science, at the University of Tampa. She specializes in research on public opinion and political psychology. Her work has been published in the *American Political Science Review*, *Journal of Politics*, *Journal of Women, Politics, and Policy*, and *Journal of Human Rights and Political Behavior*, and she is the author of three books. She lives in Tampa with her husband and three children.

Robert E. Crew Jr. is professor of political science and director of the graduate program in applied American politics at Florida State University. He has written widely on Florida politics and has managed and consulted on political campaigns in Florida and elsewhere.

Lightning Source UK Ltd.
Milton Keynes UK
UKHW02f2113040418
320528UK00007B/318/P